Terraform Cookbook
Recipes for Codifying Infrastructure

Kerim Satirli and Taylor Dolezal

Beijing · Boston · Farnham · Sebastopol · Tokyo

Terraform Cookbook

by Kerim Satirli and Taylor Dolezal

Published by O'Reilly Media, Inc., 1005 Gravenstein Highway North, Sebastopol, CA 95472.

O'Reilly books may be purchased for educational, business, or sales promotional use. Online editions are also available for most titles (*http://oreilly.com*). For more information, contact our corporate/institutional sales department: 800-998-9938 or corporate@oreilly.com.

Acquisition Editor: John Devins		**Indexer:** BIM Creatives, LLC
Development Editor: Michele Cronin		**Interior Designer:** David Futato
Production Editor: Beth Kelly		**Cover Designer:** Karen Montgomery
Copyeditor: nSight, Inc.		**Illustrator:** Kate Dullea
Proofreader: Emily Wydeven		

October 2024:   First Edition

Revision History for the First Edition

2024-10-03:   First Release

See *http://oreilly.com/catalog/errata.csp?isbn=9781098108465* for release details.

978-1-098-10846-5

[LSI]

Table of Contents

Preface

In the not-so-distant past, managing IT infrastructure was a Herculean task. System administrators juggled a dizzying array of manual processes, custom scripts, and vendor-specific tools while keeping systems running smoothly. It was an era marked by configuration drift, unexpected downtime, and the constant fear of "What if the person who set this up leaves?"

Enter the age of DevOps and infrastructure as code (IaC). This revolution gave us powerful tools to define, deploy, and manage infrastructure programmatically. At the forefront of this transformation stands HashiCorp Terraform, the most commonly used IaC tool.

With Terraform, you can describe your entire infrastructure using a declarative language. Terraform enables you to version, review, and evolve your infrastructure like any other codebase, from servers to databases to load balancers to DNS records–if there's an API for it, Terraform's vast provider ecosystem will (very likely!) be able to support it.

Instead of clicking through cloud provider consoles or writing provider-specific scripts, you can use a unified workflow across multiple clouds and services.

This cookbook is your guide to harnessing the full power of Terraform, from foundational concepts to advanced techniques and real-world applications.

Who Should Read This Book

This book is for anyone responsible for creating, managing, or improving infrastructure. That includes DevOps engineers, site reliability engineers, infrastructure developers, system administrators, and even ambitious developers looking to broaden their skills. If you've ever had to provision a server, configure a load balancer, or lose sleep over a 3 A.M. production issue, this book is for you.

We don't assume you're already an expert in infrastructure or coding. A basic familiarity with cloud concepts and comfort with the command line should suffice. Everything else you need, you'll learn along the way.

Why We Wrote This Book

As long-time practitioners and advocates of infrastructure as code, we've seen the transformative power of Terraform firsthand. But we've also experienced its learning curve and the challenges of applying it to real-world scenarios.

While the official Terraform documentation is excellent for reference, there was a clear need for a practical, recipe-based approach to learning and applying Terraform. We wanted to create a resource that not only explains the "how" but also the "why" and "when" of using Terraform effectively. This book is the result of our combined years of experience, distilled into practical, actionable recipes. It's the book we wish we had when we started our Terraform journey.

What You Will Find in This Book

Here's a brief overview of what you'll find in each chapter:

- Chapter 1 gets you started with Terraform, covering installation, basic concepts, and your first deployments.

- Chapters 2 and 3 dive deeper into Terraform syntax, functions, and best practices for writing clean, efficient code.

- Chapter 4 explores Terraform modules and providers, teaching you how to create reusable, scalable infrastructure components.

- Chapter 5 shows how to manage containers with Terraform, including deployments to Kubernetes and other orchestration platforms.

- Chapter 6 covers HCP Terraform Cloud and Enterprise, helping you understand how to use Terraform in a team setting with enhanced collaboration and governance features.

- Chapter 7 tackles the crucial topic of secret management in Terraform, ensuring your sensitive data remains secure.

- Chapters 8 and 9 delve into advanced Terraform techniques, including configuration management and complex deployment strategies.

- Finally, Chapter 10 combines real-world use cases, demonstrating how to apply everything you've learned to solve practical infrastructure challenges.

What You Won't Find in This Book

This book is definitely not a reference manual for every Terraform resource or provider. For those details, we recommend the official Terraform documentation. Instead, we focus on practical applications, best practices, and real-world scenarios that will help you become proficient with Terraform.

We've tried to make the examples as accessible as possible, primarily using AWS due to its popularity and free tier offerings. However, the principles and techniques you'll learn apply to cloud providers and services.

Conventions Used in This Book

The following typographical conventions are used in this book:

Italic
> Indicates new terms, URLs, email addresses, filenames, and file extensions.

`Constant width`
> Used for program listings, as well as within paragraphs to refer to program elements such as variable or function names, databases, data types, environment variables, statements, and keywords.

`Constant width bold`
> Shows commands or other text that should be typed literally by the user.

`Constant width italic`
> Shows text that should be replaced with user-supplied values or by values determined by context.

> This element signifies a general note.

> This element indicates a warning or caution.

Using Code Examples

Supplemental material (code examples, exercises, etc.) is available for download at *http://github.com/terraform-cookbook/recipes*. We encourage you to clone this repository and follow along with the examples as you read:

```
git clone http://github.com/terraform-cookbook/recipes.git
```

The code examples are organized by chapter, making it easy to find the relevant code for each recipe. Note that some lines of code in the book are formatted to fit the page and might include lines breaks. You can find the correctly formatted code in the GitHub repository.

If you have a technical question or a problem using the code examples, please send email to *support@oreilly.com*.

This book is here to help you get your job done. In general, if example code is offered with this book, you may use it in your programs and documentation. You do not need to contact us for permission unless you're reproducing a significant portion of the code. For example, writing a program that uses several chunks of code from this book does not require permission. Selling or distributing examples from O'Reilly books does require permission. Answering a question by citing this book and quoting example code does not require permission. Incorporating a significant amount of example code from this book into your product's documentation does require permission.

We appreciate, but generally do not require, attribution. An attribution usually includes the title, author, publisher, and ISBN. For example: "*Terraform Cookbook* by Kerim Satirli and Taylor Dolezal (O'Reilly). Copyright 2025 Hello, Operator BV and Taylor Dolezal, 978-1-098-10846-5."

If you feel your use of code examples falls outside fair use or the permission given above, feel free to contact us at *permissions@oreilly.com*.

We hope this book serves as your trusty guide in the exciting world of infrastructure as code with Terraform. May your infrastructure always be in the desired state, your deployments be swift and sure, and your "terraform apply" never need a prayer to the demo gods.

Remember, in the world of Terraform, it's not "to err is human." To err is a great opportunity to test your rollback strategy. Now go forth and `terraform apply` responsibly!

O'Reilly Online Learning

 For more than 40 years, *O'Reilly Media* has provided technology and business training, knowledge, and insight to help companies succeed.

Our unique network of experts and innovators share their knowledge and expertise through books, articles, and our online learning platform. O'Reilly's online learning platform gives you on-demand access to live training courses, in-depth learning paths, interactive coding environments, and a vast collection of text and video from O'Reilly and 200+ other publishers. For more information, visit *https://oreilly.com*.

How to Contact Us

Please address comments and questions concerning this book to the publisher:

O'Reilly Media, Inc.
1005 Gravenstein Highway North
Sebastopol, CA 95472
800-889-8969 (in the United States or Canada)
707-827-7019 (international or local)
707-829-0104 (fax)
support@oreilly.com
https://oreilly.com/about/contact.html

We have a web page for this book, where we list errata, examples, and any additional information. You can access this page at *https://oreil.ly/terraform-cookbook*.

For news and information about our books and courses, visit *https://oreilly.com*.

Find us on LinkedIn: *https://linkedin.com/company/oreilly-media*

Watch us on YouTube: *https://youtube.com/oreillymedia*

Acknowledgments

We want to express our heartfelt gratitude directly to the many individuals and groups who have contributed to the creation of this book. Your efforts have not gone unnoticed.

First and foremost, we extend our thanks to the incredible team at O'Reilly Media. Special recognition goes to Michele Cronin for her invaluable guidance and support throughout this project. We are also grateful to Beth Kelly for her expertise and to

John Devins for his assistance. Your collective efforts have significantly enhanced the quality and presentation of this book.

We thank our reviewers Rosemary Wong, Chris Devers, Werner Dijkerman, Adam McPartlan, Jess Males, Ben Muschko, and Vishwesh Shrimali. Your insightful feedback and suggestions have been instrumental in refining and improving the content of this book. Your expertise and time are greatly appreciated.

Last but certainly not least, we want to acknowledge the vibrant Terraform community. This book, like Terraform itself, owes its existence to the collective knowledge, creativity, and passion of countless individuals. Your significant contributions, whether through code, documentation, or shared experiences, have not only shaped this book but the entire Terraform ecosystem. We are all better because of this community's collaborative spirit and dedication.

To everyone who has been a part of this journey, whether mentioned here by name or not, thank you. Your support, encouragement, and expertise have made *Terraform Cookbook* possible.

## CHAPTER 1

Getting Started with Terraform

Terraform is a source-available tool created by HashiCorp that allows you to manage your infrastructure as code (IaC). It provides a simple and consistent way to define, provision, and manage resources across cloud platforms and on-premises environments.

With Terraform, you can describe your infrastructure in a declarative language called the HashiCorp configuration language (HCL). This allows you to specify the desired state of your infrastructure rather than having to script the steps to get there. Terraform then applies this configuration to create, modify, or delete resources as necessary to achieve the desired state.

The real power of Terraform is in its ability to manage complex infrastructure. You can create reusable modules that can be shared and applied to different projects, making it easy to maintain consistency across multiple environments. Additionally, Terraform's state management system ensures that the current state of your infrastructure is tracked and can be used to update, destroy, or re-create resources as needed.

One of the significant benefits of using Terraform is its support for a wide range of cloud providers, such as Amazon Web Services (AWS), Google Cloud Platform (GCP), and Microsoft Azure. This allows you to manage your infrastructure across different providers, avoiding vendor lock-in and providing greater flexibility. Terraform is widely used for cloud infrastructure and supports many noncloud-specific providers, such as Kubernetes, GitLab, and PostgreSQL. Its capabilities extend beyond cloud deployments to support hybrid and on-premises environments, including bare-metal hardware servers.

Terraform is a powerful tool for reducing the friction around managing IaC, deploying, maintaining, and scaling your applications. With Terraform, you can describe your infrastructure using a simple and consistent language, reuse modules, and manage resources across different providers.

This book is for infrastructure engineers, DevOps professionals, and cloud architects who want to learn how to effectively manage infrastructure as code using Terraform. Whether you're new to infrastructure as code or looking to improve your Terraform skills, this book will walk you through practical examples and best practices to help you confidently deploy and manage infrastructure across different environments.

It's important to note that in August 2023, HashiCorp changed Terraform's license from the Mozilla Public License (MPL) to the Business Source License (BSL). This change sparked significant discussion in the open source community and led to the creation of OpenTofu, an open source fork of Terraform that remains under the MPL. The BSL allows for most open source use cases but restricts using Terraform as a competing product or service. While this book focuses on HashiCorp's Terraform, we have written our examples, concepts, and practices to work with OpenTofu as well. Users should be aware of these licensing changes and consider their implications when choosing between Terraform and OpenTofu for their projects.

1.1 When to Use Terraform

Terraform is an excellent choice when managing complex infrastructure composed of many resources. It's beneficial when managing infrastructure that spans multiple cloud providers or on-premises environments. Here are some examples of when to use Terraform:

Managing multiple environments
Terraform excels at managing multiple environments, such as development, staging, and production. With Terraform, you can define your infrastructure as code, making it easy to deploy and manage across environments.

Managing complex infrastructure
Terraform is particularly useful for managing complex infrastructure composed of many resources. With Terraform, you can define your infrastructure in a declarative language, creating, modifying, and deleting resources.

Managing infrastructure across cloud providers
Terraform is an excellent choice for managing infrastructure across different cloud providers. With Terraform, you can consistently define your infrastructure, regardless of your cloud provider.

Automating infrastructure deployment
Terraform is an excellent choice for automating infrastructure deployment. With Terraform, you can define your infrastructure as code and use automation tools, such as CI/CD pipelines, to deploy your infrastructure automatically.

1.2 When Not to Use Terraform

While Terraform is a powerful tool, some jobs have better choices. Here are some examples of when you might want to consider other tools:

Single-server infrastructure
> If you manage a single server, you might not need Terraform. Simple configuration management tools such as Ansible or Puppet might be a better choice.

Infrastructure as a service (IaaS)
> If you only use a single cloud provider and manage only a small amount of infrastructure, you might not need Terraform. Many cloud providers offer tools for managing infrastructure, such as AWS CloudFormation or Azure Resource Manager.

Platform as a service (PaaS)
> If you use a service like Netlify or Google App Engine, you might not need Terraform. These providers typically manage the infrastructure for you, so you only need to worry about deploying your application.

When deciding whether to use Terraform, consider the complexity of your infrastructure and whether you need to manage infrastructure across multiple providers. Consider other tools if you manage only a small amount of infrastructure or use only a single cloud provider.

Unique or specialized systems. In some cases, particularly in medium to large organizations, specialized systems or departments with unique needs might not fit nicely into a standardized infrastructure-as-code approach. For example, manual configuration or more straightforward scripting tools might better serve a research lab with custom equipment or a department with legacy systems. However, if your organization has broadly adopted an infrastructure-as-code mindset, it's worth considering whether these "snowflake" systems could benefit from being managed with code. This approach could provide consistency, ease of redeployment, and better integration with your overall infrastructure management strategy. The decision often depends on the specific needs of the system, the skills of the team managing it, and your organization's overall infrastructure philosophy.

1.3 Installing and Configuring Terraform

Problem

You need to install Terraform on your local machine or a remote server.

Solution

Use the appropriate installation method for your operating system or package manager.

Here are the steps for installing Terraform on some popular operating systems:

Installing Terraform on Linux

Many Linux distributions offer Terraform in their official package repositories. For example, on Debian/Ubuntu systems, you can install Terraform using:

```
sudo apt update
sudo apt install terraform
```

On Red Hat-based systems, you can use:

```
sudo yum install terraform
```

If your distribution doesn't offer Terraform or you need a specific version, follow these manual installation steps:

1. Download the latest Terraform package for Linux from the official Terraform website (*https://oreil.ly/OILYx*).

2. Extract the downloaded package to a directory on your system. For example, `sudo unzip terraform_1.9.2_linux_amd64.zip -d /usr/local/bin/`.

3. Make the Terraform binary executable by running `sudo chmod +x /usr/local/bin/terraform`.

4. Verify the installation by running `terraform version`.

Installing Terraform on macOS

Homebrew is a popular package manager for macOS, but it's not included by default. If you don't have Homebrew installed, install it from *https://brew.sh* before proceeding with these instructions:

1. Install Terraform using Homebrew by running:

   ```
   brew tap hashicorp/tap
   brew install hashicorp/tap/terraform
   ```

2. Verify the installation by running:

   ```
   terraform version
   ```

Installing Terraform on Windows

Follow these steps:

1. Download the latest Terraform package for Windows from the official Terraform website (*https://oreil.ly/OILYx*).

2. Extract the downloaded package to a directory on your system.

3. Add the directory containing the Terraform executable to your system's PATH environment variable.

4. Verify the installation by running `terraform version`.

Installing OpenTofu

OpenTofu, the open source fork of Terraform, can be installed using similar methods. Here are the installation steps for different operating systems:

Linux
> You can use the official OpenTofu install script:
>
> ```
> curl --proto '=https' --tlsv1.2 -fsSL https://get.opentofu.org/install-opentofu.sh | sh
> ```
>
> Alternatively, you can download the binary from the OpenTofu GitHub releases page, extract it, and move it to your PATH.

macOS
> Using Homebrew:
>
> ```
> brew install opentofu
> ```
>
> You can also use the official install script or download the binary described in the Linux instructions.

Windows
> You can use Chocolatey:
>
> ```
> choco install opentofu
> ```
>
> Alternatively, download the Windows binary from the GitHub releases page, extract it, and add it to your PATH.
>
> After installation, you can verify the installation by running:
>
> ```
> tofu version
> ```

OpenTofu uses the `tofu` command instead of `terraform` to avoid conflicts if both are installed on the same system.

Remember that while the installation processes for Terraform and OpenTofu are different, the usage and syntax are nearly identical. The examples in this book will work with both tools, with the main difference being the command used (`terraform` versus `tofu`).

Discussion

Terraform and OpenTofu are available for various operating systems and can be installed through multiple methods, including package managers, official installers, and manual installation from binaries. The choice of installation method often depends on your specific needs and system configuration.

Package managers such as Advanced Packaging Tool (APT), Yellowdog Updater Modified (YUM), and Homebrew offer the most straightforward installation process and automatically handle tasks like adding executables to your PATH. They also make it easy to update to newer versions. However, they may not always offer the latest version immediately after release.

Manual installation from binaries gives you more control over the exact version you're installing and where it's placed on your system. This can be useful in environments where you must run multiple versions or have specific system requirements. However, it requires more hands-on management, including manually updating your PATH and handling upgrades.

The installation process for OpenTofu is similar to Terraform, with the main difference being the source of the binaries and the command used (`tofu` instead of `terraform`). This allows you to have both installed on the same system without conflicts.

When installing either tool, verifying the installation by checking the version number is essential. This confirms a successful installation and lets you know the exact version you're working with, which can be crucial when following tutorials or troubleshooting issues.

While Terraform and OpenTofu have different installation processes, their usage and syntax are nearly identical. The examples and concepts in this book apply to both tools, with the primary difference being the command invocation (`terraform` versus `tofu`).

Regardless of which tool or installation method you choose, understanding the basics of the installation process can be helpful for troubleshooting, upgrading, or setting up development environments. As methods may change, always refer to the official documentation (see Figure 1-1) for the most up-to-date installation instructions.

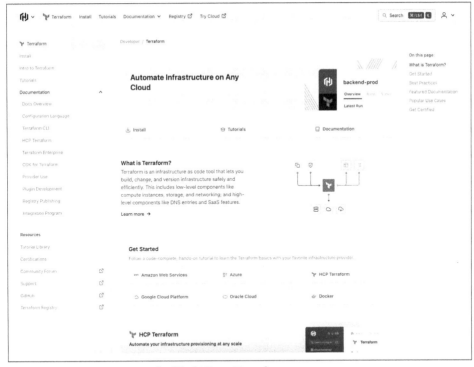

Figure 1-1. Documentation for HashiCorp Terraform

1.4 Understanding Terraform Providers

Problem

You want to start using Terraform providers in your IaC projects, but you don't know where to begin or how to configure your providers properly.

Solution

To start using Terraform providers, you need to follow these steps:

1. Choose the provider(s) you want to use. Searching the Terraform Registry (*https://oreil.ly/fgQdz*) is a great place to see all your available provider options.

2. Add the provider(s) to your Terraform configuration file (e.g., *main.tf*).

3. Configure the provider(s) with required settings, such as API keys or authentication tokens.

4. Use the provider(s) in your Terraform resources.

Examples in this book will consist of various clouds, though we will use AWS for many of them, as it's one of the more popular cloud providers and Terraform Registry downloads.

Here's an example of how to add and configure the `aws` provider:

```
# Step 1: Choose the provider (AWS)
provider "aws" {}

# Step 2: Configure the provider with any required settings
provider "aws" {
  region     = "us-west-2"
  access_key = "YOUR_ACCESS_KEY"
  secret_key = "YOUR_SECRET_KEY"
}

# Step 3: Use the provider to create resources

Provider "aws" {

  ...

}

resource "aws_instance" "example" {
  ami           = "ami-0c55b159cbfafe1f0"
  instance_type = "t2.micro"
}
```

In this example, we've chosen the `aws` provider and added it to our configuration file using the `provider` block. We've configured the `provider` with a `region` setting and provided AWS `access_key` and `secret_key` in the `provider` block.

We can then use the `aws_instance` resource to create an EC2 instance, specifying the `ami` and `instance_type` settings.

Discussion

Terraform providers are plug-ins that allow Terraform to interact with different cloud services or other external APIs. The community and the Terraform team maintain providers and can be found in the Terraform Registry.

To choose a provider, visit the Terraform Registry and find the provider you want to use. Each provider has a page with installation instructions, usage examples, and a list of available resources.

You'll need a `provider` block to add a provider to your Terraform configuration file. This block tells Terraform which provider to use and how to configure it.

The provider block specifies the provider type (in this case, `aws`) and any provider-specific settings (in this case, the `region`, `access_key`, and `secret_key` variables). You can add as many distinct provider blocks as needed in your configuration file (e.g., `aws`, `kubernetes`, `helm`, etc.).

Some providers require configuring additional settings, such as API keys or authentication tokens. These settings can be specified in the provider block.

Once you've added and configured your provider(s), you can use them in your Terraform resources. Each provider has a set of resources that you can use to create and manage infrastructure.

The aws provider supplies resources for creating EC2 instances, security groups, and many other AWS resources. We created an aws_instance resource with the identifier example in this example. We've specified the ami and instance_type settings for the instance, though many more arguments can be specified and set for the aws_instance resource.

You can download the necessary provider plug-ins and initialize your configuration using the Terraform init command. Once your configuration is initialized, you can use the terraform plan and terraform apply commands to create or modify your infrastructure.

You now know how to start using Terraform providers in your IaC projects. Happy provisioning!

1.5 Understanding Terraform Modules

Problem

You need to create a new Amazon Virtual Private Cloud (VPC) with a specific Classless Inter-Domain Routing (CIDR) block, subnets, and internet gateway, but you don't want to start creating this from scratch.

Solution

In this solution, we leverage a prebuilt Terraform module to effortlessly provision a VPC along with its associated resources such as subnets and an internet gateway. This approach saves time and ensures conformity to best practices:

```
module "vpc" {
  source  = "terraform-aws-modules/vpc/aws"
  version = "3.19.0"

  name = "my-vpc"
  cidr = "10.0.0.0/16"

  azs = ["us-west-2a", "us-west-2b", "us-west-2c"]
  private_subnets = ["10.0.1.0/24", "10.0.2.0/24", "10.0.3.0/24"]
  public_subnets  = ["10.0.101.0/24", "10.0.102.0/24", "10.0.103.0/24"]

  enable_nat_gateway = true

  tags = {
    Terraform   = "true"
```

```
    Environment = "dev"
  }
}
```

Discussion

We used a Terraform module called vpc, sourced from the `terraform-aws-modules` `/vpc/aws` module. The module takes several inputs, including the VPC's name, CIDR block, availability zones, subnets, NAT gateway, and tags.

The `name` input specifies the name of the VPC, while the `cidr` input specifies the CIDR block to use for the VPC. We've chosen a CIDR block of 10.0.0.0/16 in this example.

The `azs` input specifies the availability zones to use for the VPC. In this example, we've chosen three availability zones in the western United States (Oregon) region.

The `private_subnets` and `public_subnets` inputs specify the CIDR blocks for the VPC's private and public subnets, respectively. In this example, we've chosen three private and three public subnets.

The `enable_nat_gateway` input specifies whether or not to create a NAT gateway for the VPC. In this example, we've set this input to `true`.

Finally, the `tags` input specifies any additional tags to apply to the VPC resources.

Once you've defined the `vpc` module in your Terraform configuration, you can apply it by running `terraform apply`. Terraform will then create the VPC, subnets, and other resources defined in the module.

1.6 Modifying Terraform State with terraform console

Problem

You need to modify Terraform state manually for testing or debugging purposes.

Solution

Modify Terraform state with the following steps:

1. Navigate to the directory containing your Terraform configuration files.

2. Run the command `terraform console`.

3. The `terraform console` prompt will appear.

4. Enter the command `state.<module-name>.<resource-name>.<attribute-name>` to load the current Terraform state into the console, where `<module-name>`,

---

`<resource-name>`, or `<attribute-name>` are the names of the module, resource, and attribute you want to view.

5. The current value of the attribute will be displayed.

Discussion

The `terraform console` is a powerful tool that allows you to modify Terraform state using HCL interactively. This is useful for testing or debugging, as it will enable you to introspect your Terraform's state without modifying the Terraform configuration files.

To use `terraform console`, navigate to the directory containing your Terraform configuration files and run the command `terraform console`. This will open an interactive console that allows you to execute HCL expressions.

To modify a specific attribute in your Terraform state, you need to load the attribute into the console using the `state.<module-name>.<resource-name>.<attribute-name>` syntax. This will display the attribute's current value, and you can modify it using HCL syntax. Once you've modified the value, press Enter to apply the change to the Terraform state.

Modifying Terraform state manually using `terraform console` should only be done for testing or debugging purposes and *should not be used* in production environments. Modifying the state manually can cause unexpected results and may put your infrastructure at risk.

1.7 Using HashiCorp Cloud Platform Terraform

Problem

You want to store your Terraform state in a secure location that is accessible for both you and any additional team members you work with.

Solution

Use HashiCorp Cloud Platform Terraform (HCP Terraform; formerly Terraform Cloud) as a remote backend to store your Terraform state. To do this, you must configure your Terraform code to use HCP Terraform as the backend, then initialize Terraform to use this backend.

Here's an example of how to configure your Terraform code to use HCP Terraform as the backend:

```
terraform {
  cloud {
    organization = "<your-organization-name>"

    workspaces {
      name = "<your-workspace-name>"
    }
  }
}
```

 Replace *<your-organization-name>* and *<your-workspace-name>* with your organization and workspace names in HCP Terraform.

Once you've added this configuration to your Terraform code, you can initialize Terraform to use the backend by running the following commands:

```
terraform init -backend-config="token=<HCP Terraform API token>"
```

 Replace *<HCP Terraform API token>* with your HCP Terraform API token. You can find your API token in the HCP Terraform UI under User Settings → Tokens.

While this example uses HCP Terraform, it's important to note that Terraform supports various backend types for storing state. Some popular alternatives include:

Amazon S3
Stores the state as a key in an S3 bucket with an optional DynamoDB table for state locking

Azure Blob Storage
Stores the state in Azure Blob Storage accounts

Google Cloud Storage
Stores the state in a Google Cloud Storage bucket

Consul
Stores the state in Consul Key/Value store (*https://oreil.ly/eSnin*)

Local
Stores the state on the local filesystem (this is not recommended for team environments)

Discussion

Storing your Terraform state in a remote location is a best practice for managing infrastructure as code, and it's easy to set up by utilizing the commands listed in this recipe. It ensures that your state is centralized and accessible from anywhere. It provides additional security by keeping your state out of version control systems and on infrastructure where secrets can be accessed.

HCP Terraform is a popular choice for storing Terraform state remotely, as it provides a secure and managed backend that is explicitly designed for Terraform. To use HCP Terraform as a backend, you must configure your Terraform code to use the remote backend type and specify your organization and workspace names. You can specify other backend configurations, such as encryption and state versioning.

While we've focused on HCP Terraform in this example, the principles of remote state storage apply to other backend types as well. The choice of backend depends on your specific needs, existing infrastructure, and organizational policies. HCP Terraform provides a managed solution that's tightly integrated with other HashiCorp products, but other cloud storage solutions or self-hosted options such as Consul can be equally effective when properly configured.

1.8 Using Terraform with Visual Studio Code

Problem

You want to use Terraform with Visual Studio Code (VS Code) to write and manage your IaC projects.

Solution

To use Terraform with VS Code, you need to follow this process.

If you haven't already, download and install VS Code from the Visual Studio Code website (*https://oreil.ly/OtIHF*).

Install the Terraform extension for VS Code by doing the following:

1. Open Visual Studio Code.
2. Open the Extensions view by clicking the Extensions icon in the sidebar or pressing Ctrl + Shift + X on Windows or Cmd + Shift + X on macOS.
3. Search for the `hashicorp.terraform` extension.
4. Click the Install button to install the extension (see Figure 1-2).

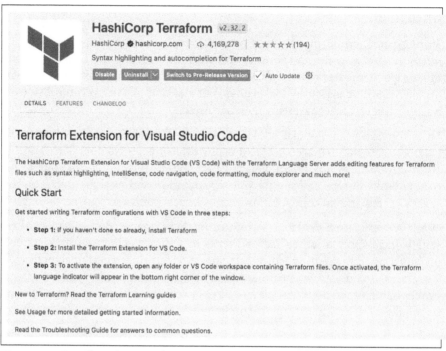

Figure 1-2. Installing the Terraform extension for Visual Studio Code

Open a directory containing any of your Terraform projects in VS Code. You can even use the integrated terminal to run Terraform commands.

Discussion

VS Code's editing features can be used to write and format your Terraform code. The Terraform extension provides syntax highlighting, code completion, and linting features to help you write correct and well-structured code.

The Terraform extension provides several features to help you manage your project, such as:

Run Terraform commands
> You can use the integrated terminal to run Terraform commands, such as `terraform init`, `terraform plan`, and `terraform apply`.

Preview changes
> You can use the Terraform extension to preview changes to your infrastructure before applying them. Click the Terraform icon in the sidebar and select Show Terraform Output.

View resources
> You can view your infrastructure resources using the Terraform extension. Click the Terraform icon in the sidebar and select Show Terraform Graph.

1.9 Managing Terraform Provider Version Constraints

Problem

You need to manage the version constraints of your Terraform providers to ensure that you have certainty in the ability to reproduce your IaC instantiations.

Solution

Use the `version` argument in your provider configuration to specify the desired provider version and use version constraints to manage which provider versions are acceptable.

Here's an example of how to specify a provider version and version constraint in your Terraform code:

```
provider "aws" {
  version = "~> 5.0"
  region  = "us-west-2"
}
```

In this example, the `version` argument specifies a version constraint of `~> 5.0`, which means that any version of the provider greater than or equal to `5.0` and less than `6.0` will be accepted. This allows you to automatically upgrade to the latest version of the provider within the `5.x` range, but prevents upgrades to `6.0` or higher, which may introduce breaking changes.

You can also specify an exact version of the provider by setting the version argument to a specific version number, like this:

```
provider "aws" {
  version = "5.1.0"
  region  = "us-west-2"
}
```

In this example, only version `5.1.0` of the provider will be accepted.

Discussion

Managing the version constraints of your Terraform providers is an essential part of IaC, as it allows you to ensure that your infrastructure is deployed using a known and tested version of each provider. By specifying version constraints in your provider configuration, you can ensure that you are using a version of the provider that is compatible with your infrastructure code.

Generally, it is recommended to use version constraints that allow for automatic upgrades within a given range but prevent upgrades to higher major versions. This will enable you to take advantage of new features and bug fixes within a given version range but prevents breaking changes from being introduced by major version upgrades.

By specifying version constraints in your provider configuration, you can also prevent unexpected or accidental upgrades of your provider versions. This can help to avoid issues caused by breaking changes introduced by new provider versions.

Managing the version constraints of your Terraform providers is an integral part of infrastructure as code. By using the `version` argument in your provider configuration and specifying version constraints, you can ensure that you use the correct provider version for your infrastructure, prevent unexpected upgrades, and take advantage of new features and bug fixes within a given version range.

While version constraints in your configuration help control which provider versions are acceptable, Terraform also uses a dependency lock file (`.terraform.lock.hcl`) to record the exact versions of providers used in your project. This file, created or updated when you run `terraform init`, ensures consistency across team members and environments, enables reproducibility, and prevents automatic updates to new provider versions even if they satisfy your constraints. Here's an example of a lock file entry:

```
provider "registry.terraform.io/hashicorp/aws" {
  version     = "5.67.0"
  constraints = "~> 5.0"
  hashes = [
    "h1:z1+WjdwuRX8Aa9a7YKXErhZ5AuvoXiDq7FHts30sZak=",
    # ... other hashes ...
  ]
}
```

Use `terraform init- upgrade` to upgrade to a newer version within your constraints. It's a good practice to commit the lock file to version control and your Terraform configuration files, ensuring infrastructure consistency across different environments and team members.

1.10 Strategies for Deploying Version-Controlled Terraform Code Repositories

Problem

Deploying IaC using Terraform necessitates an organized, version-controlled approach to manage code iterations and ensure reproducibility and traceability. Leveraging version control systems (VCS) like Git and GitOps practices allow for systematic, automated, and auditable infrastructure deployment. Identifying recommended approaches and best practices in this domain is crucial for ensuring smooth deployment pipelines and operational efficiency.

Solution

Learn how to set up version-controlled Terraform and set up some branch protection to ensure that only valid Terraform code gets applied:

```
module "vcs_repo" {
  source = "git::https://github.corp/platform/terraform-github-repos.git?ref=v1.0.0"
}

provider "github" {
  token        = var.github_token
  organization = var.github_organization
}

resource "github_repository" "terraform_repo" {
  name        = "terraform-repo"
  description = "Terraform repository for managing infrastructure"
}

resource "github_branch_protection" "main" {
  repository     = github_repository.terraform_repo.name
  pattern        = "main"
  enforce_admins = false

  required_status_checks {
    strict   = true
    contexts = ["ci/terraform-run"]
  }
}
```

Discussion

In the solution provided, we delineate a typical setup where a Terraform module is sourced from a version-controlled repository and utilized within a GitHub organization to manage infrastructure deployments:

Module source versioning
> The module block sources a specific version (v1.0.0) of a Terraform module from a Git repository. By referencing a particular version, you ensure the reproducibility of your infrastructure deployments.

GitHub provider configuration
> The provider block configures the GitHub provider with credentials and organizational context. This setup is crucial for interfacing with GitHub to manage repositories and other GitHub resources.

GitHub repository resource
> The resource "github_repository" block creates a new GitHub repository named terraform-repo, designated for managing Terraform code.

Branch protection

The resource `"github_branch_protection"` block sets up branch protection rules for the main branch of the `terraform-repo`. Enforcing status checks from a CI/CD pipeline such as GitHub Actions ensures that proposed changes pass necessary validation before merging.

The encapsulated GitOps approach within this setup fosters a culture of monitoring and validating changes in a version-controlled manner before applying them to the infrastructure. This structure enables collaboration and code sharing via module versioning, ensuring a systematic, traceable deployment workflow.

1.11 Deploying a Docker Container with Terraform

Problem

You want to use Terraform to manage and run your Docker containers on your machine or a Docker host.

Solution

Use the Docker provider in Terraform to manage your Docker containers and run them on your Docker host. The Docker provider allows you to define containers, images, and networks in your Terraform code and then apply that code to create or update your infrastructure.

Here's an example of how to use the Docker provider to run a container:

```
provider "docker" {}

resource "docker_container" "example" {
  name  = "example"
  image = "nginx"
  ports {
    internal = 80
    external = 8000
  }
}
```

In this example, the `docker_container` resource defines a container named `example` that uses the `nginx` image and maps port `80` inside the container to port `8000` on the host.

To apply this configuration and create the container, run the following commands:

1. Initialize Terraform by running `terraform init`.

2. Apply the configuration by running `terraform apply`.

This will create the container on your Docker host and map port 80 inside the container to port 8000 on the host. You can then access the nginx web server running inside the container by visiting `http://localhost:8000` in your web browser.

Discussion

The Docker provider is a powerful tool that allows you to manage your Docker containers using Terraform. By defining containers, images, and networks in your Terraform code, you can ensure that your Docker infrastructure is version controlled and reproducible.

Note that you'll need to install Docker on your machine or host. Once you install Docker, you can initialize the `docker` provider in your Terraform code by adding a provider block.

Using Terraform resources, you can then define Docker resources, such as containers and images. Each resource has configuration options, like the container name and the image to use, allowing you to customize your Docker use cases.

Once you've defined your Docker resources, you can apply the configuration to create or update your infrastructure. Terraform will communicate with the Docker API to create or modify your containers, images, and networks.

1.12 Upgrading Terraform: From 0.x to 1.x and Beyond

Problem

You are using an older version of Terraform (0.15 or earlier) and need to upgrade to the latest 1.x version. While many users have already made this transition, understanding the upgrade process is crucial for maintaining legacy systems or joining projects that may still use older versions.

Solution

Upgrading from legacy versions of Terraform must be a measured process and has to be done step-by-step:

1. Create a backup of your Terraform state file(s) in case you need to restore to a previous version of the state file manually.

2. Determine if you are running the latest version of your current major version. For example, if you are on `v0.12`, make sure you are on `v0.12.31`, the latest `0.12` version of Terraform at the time of writing.

3. Update to the latest version of `v0.13` and run the upgrade command `terraform 0.13upgrade` to make a best-effort upgrade to your code with version-specific syntax changes in mind.

4. Following the upgrade command, inspect your code and verify line-by-line that all changes are intentional.

 Terraform upgrade commands make the best effort to update structures to a more modern version whenever possible. When the upgrade logic cannot determine the best path forward, a comment usually indicates which steps you must take manually.

5. When all changes look satisfactory, use the Terraform Plan and Apply approach until you can verify that the upgrade has been completed.

At this point, revert to step 1, create a new backup of your Terraform state file(s), then continue the process (but increment each version).

Once you have updated your code to Terraform `v0.14.0` or later, continue the upgrade process as usual by simply installing a newer version of Terraform.

Next, use the Terraform Plan and Apply approach until you can verify that the upgrade for the current version you are upgrading to has been completed.

Discussion

Upgrading to newer Terraform versions from its predecessors has traditionally been a meticulous task, necessitating a thorough review to prevent the introduction of breaking changes in an infrastructure environment. This has often made version upgrades a labor-intensive endeavor.

However, a significant turn came with the release of Terraform v0.15, followed by Terraform 1.0. HashiCorp rolled out a set of compatibility guarantees for the entire Terraform v1.x life cycle. These guarantees address substantial backward compatibility considerations encompassing a wide range of Terraform functions, language features, changes to the wire protocol, and other elements that could adversely impact the operator experience.

The essence of this compatibility promise is to prevent the introduction of breaking changes by HashiCorp. Nevertheless, it's imperative for you, as a Terraform codebase operator, to stay updated with relatively recent releases of Terraform.

A practical guideline is to lag by no more than two minor versions—translating to approximately a 9–12 month lag from the latest released version. For instance, if the prevailing Terraform version is v1.6.0, it's advisable to be on v1.4.0 or a newer version.

We strongly advocate for a proactive approach toward testing and transitioning to contemporary Terraform versions. This not only ensures access to essential bug fixes but also to significant security enhancements.

1.13 Using Terraform Variables

Problem

You want to create abstractions in your Terraform code to make it more modular and reusable.

Solution

Use Terraform variables to create abstractions in your Terraform code. Variables allow you to parameterize your Terraform code and make it more flexible, allowing you to reuse the same code in different contexts.

Here's an example of how to use variables to create an abstraction in your Terraform code:

```
variable "region" {
  type    = string
  default = "us-west-1"
}

provider "aws" {
  region = var.region
}

resource "aws_instance" "example" {
  ami           = "ami-0c55b159cbfafe1f0"
  instance_type = "t2.micro"
  region        = var.region
}
```

To use this configuration with a different region, simply override the `region` variable value when applying the configuration:

```
terraform apply -var region=us-east-1
```

Discussion

Using variables is a powerful way to create abstractions in your Terraform code. By parameterizing your code, you can make it more flexible and reusable, allowing you to use the same code in different contexts with different values for the variables.

In this example, the `region` variable is used to parameterize the region value for the `aws` provider and the `aws_instance` resource. Using a variable for the region allows you to reuse the same code with different region values easily.

Variables can also create more complex abstractions, such as modules. Modules are a way to encapsulate Terraform code and construct reusable, shareable components. Modules can take input variables and output values, allowing you to create more complex abstractions that can be used in different contexts.

When using variables, it's essential to be careful about the scope and visibility of the variable. You should avoid using global variables that can be accessed from anywhere in your Terraform code, as this can make your code harder to understand and maintain. Instead, use variables that are scoped to specific modules or resources and pass values between them using input and output variables.

1.14 Consistent Code for a Consistent Experience

Problem

When managing IaC with Terraform, it's imperative to have a well-defined workflow that ensures consistency, repeatability, and ease of collaboration among team members. Understanding the typical Terraform workflow and adhering to best practices is essential for managing infrastructure effectively and ensuring a uniform experience across various environments.

Solution

Utilizing the `required_version` directive ensures specific versions of either Terraform or Terraform modules:

```
terraform {
  required_version = ">= 1.0.0"

  cloud {
    hostname     = "app.terraform.io"
    organization = "example-org"

    workspaces {
      name = "my-workspace"
    }
  }
}

provider "aws" {
  region = "us-west-2"
}

resource "aws_instance" "example" {
  ami           = "ami-abcdefgh"
  instance_type = "t2.micro"
}
```

Discussion

Here are aspects of the code:

Version constraint

The `required_version` directive in the `terraform` block specifies the version of Terraform required for this configuration. Selecting a version constraint is a good practice to ensure consistency across different environments and team members.

Backend configuration

The `backend "remote"` block configures a remote backend for storing the Terraform state. Remote backends like HCP Terraform or Terraform Enterprise provide a centralized way to store and manage Terraform state, enabling collaboration and consistency.

Provider configuration

The `provider "aws"` block specifies the provider and its configuration. Keeping provider configurations consistent ensures the same behavior across different environments and team members.

Resource configuration

The `resource "aws_instance" "example"` block defines an AWS EC2 instance. Consistently structuring resource blocks and following naming conventions are essential for readable, maintainable, and collaborative code.

The outlined Terraform configuration and workflow encapsulate several best practices for maintaining a consistent experience when managing infrastructure as code. Adhering to a standardized workflow, defining explicit version constraints, utilizing remote backends for state management, and maintaining a consistent provider and resource configuration are critical steps toward achieving a uniform, predictable infrastructure management experience.

Terraform Basics

It's an understatement to say that there are many ways in which folks can use Terraform. From standing up GitHub organizations, provisioning their cluster management solution, to even curating the perfect Spotify playlist, Terraform is an excellent, declarative way to manage many things, even though it's not always apparent what the best practices are for writing Terraform or how to construct your code. We'll dig into the basics of Terraform in this chapter.

2.1 Formatting and Validating Terraform Code

Problem

You have written some Terraform code, which is hard to read and understand. It needs to be formatted consistently, and you want to ensure the code is valid before applying it.

Solution

The first step in the solution is to run the `terraform fmt` command, which allows for real-time evaluation of Terraform expressions:

```
# Step 1: Run the Terraform format command
terraform fmt

# Step 2: Run the Terraform validate command
terraform init
terraform validate
```

Discussion

The `terraform fmt` command automatically formats your Terraform code to follow the recommended style guidelines, making it easier to read and maintain. This command should be run in the same directory as your Terraform configuration files.

The `terraform validate` command checks the syntax and semantics of your Terraform code to ensure that it's valid before applying it. It checks for syntax errors, missing required arguments, and incorrect references. However, it does not check if the configuration will produce the desired infrastructure.

Note that before running `terraform validate`, you need to run `terraform init`. This is because validation requires context from the providers, while formatting is a generic operation that doesn't need provider information.

2.2 Rapid Experimentation with terraform console

Problem

You want to quickly test and experiment with Terraform functions, expressions, or interpolation without modifying your configuration files.

Solution

Start your rapid experimentation journey by running the `terraform console` command:

```
# Step 1: Start the Terraform console
terraform console

# Step 2: Experiment with Terraform expressions
> 2 + 3
5
> join(",", ["a", "b", "c"])
"a,b,c"
> lookup({a="foo", b="bar"}, "a", "default")
"foo"
```

Discussion

The `terraform console` command provides an interactive console that allows you to evaluate Terraform expressions, functions, and interpolation. This tool is helpful for rapid experimentation and debugging without affecting your existing configuration files.

When you run `terraform console`, it starts an interactive read-eval-print loop (REPL) session in your terminal. You can type Terraform expressions or functions; the console will evaluate them and display the results.

Remember that the `terraform console` command uses the current workspace's state, so any resources or outputs defined in your configuration will be accessible within the console. This is helpful for testing expressions that reference existing resources or variables.

Here's what's happening in our examples:

- `2 + 3` demonstrates basic arithmetic.
- `join(",", ["a", "b", "c"])` shows string manipulation.
- `lookup({a="foo", b="bar"}, "a", "default")` illustrates working with maps.

These simple examples show how to quickly test Terraform functions and expressions without modifying your main configuration files.

2.3 Improving Code Quality with TFLint

Problem

You want to improve the quality of your Terraform code by detecting potential issues not caught by the built-in `terraform validate` command. For example, you want to identify deprecated syntax or provider-specific best practices.

Solution

Elevate your Terraform development process by installing TFLint, a linter that provides immediate feedback on code quality and potential errors:

```
# Step 1: Install TFLint (for Linux amd64, adjust as needed for your OS)
curl -L "$(curl -Ls https://api.github.com/repos/terraform-linters/tflint/releases/latest | grep -o -E
   "https://.+?_linux_amd64.zip")" -o tflint.zip && unzip tflint.zip && sudo mv tflint /usr/local/bin/
      && rm tflint.zip

# Step 2: Run TFLint on your Terraform code
tflint
```

Discussion

TFLint is a third-party linting tool for Terraform code that helps you identify and fix issues not caught by Terraform's built-in validation. It can detect unused variables, duplicate resources, and incorrect resource properties.

For instance, TFLint can identify issues such as:

- Use of deprecated resource attributes
- Violation of AWS-specific naming conventions

- Potential security risks, such as overly permissive security group rules
- Inconsistencies between variable types and their usage

Before using TFLint, you need to install it. The provided command in the solution downloads the latest TFLint release for Linux from GitHub, unzips the archive, moves the binary to /usr/local/bin, and removes the zip file. Visit the official installation guide (*https://oreil.ly/8k-wu*) for other platforms or installation methods.

Once installed, you can run tflint in the same directory as your Terraform configuration files. By default, TFLint will check all *.tf* files in the current directory and output any issues it finds.

Using TFLint in combination with Terraform's built-in validation and formatting commands helps improve the quality of your Terraform code, making it more readable, maintainable, and less prone to errors. Consider integrating TFLint into your CI/CD pipeline or Git precommit hooks to automatically check your Terraform code before it's committed or deployed.

2.4 Improving Code Quality with TFSec

Problem

You want to improve the security of your Terraform code by identifying and fixing potential security issues that may not be caught by Terraform's built-in validation or other linting tools.

Solution

Implement this code:

```
# Step 1: Install TFSec (for Linux amd64, adjust as needed for your OS)
curl -L "$(curl -Ls https://api.github.com/repos/tfsec/tfsec/releases/latest | grep -o -E "https://.+?
_linux_amd64.tar.gz")" -o tfsec.tar.gz && tar -xzf tfsec.tar.gz && sudo mv tfsec /usr/local/bin/ &&
  rm tfsec.tar.gz

# Step 2: Run TFSec on your Terraform code
tfsec
```

Discussion

TFSec is a third-party security scanner for Terraform code that helps you identify and fix potential security issues not caught by Terraform's built-in validation or other linting tools. It scans your Terraform configuration files for insecure patterns, misconfigurations, and noncompliant settings, providing recommendations to improve security.

For instance, TFSec can identify issues such as:

- Unencrypted S3 buckets
- Security groups with overly permissive ingress rules
- Use of default virtual private clouds (VPCs)
- Unencrypted Amazon Elastic Block Store (EBS) volumes

You can ignore specific checks directly in your Terraform files by adding comments. For example:

```
#tfsec:ignore:aws-iam-no-policy-wildcards resource "aws_iam_policy" "example" { # ... }
```

This tells TFSec to ignore the `aws-iam-no-policy-wildcards` check for this specific resource. Use this sparingly and always document why a check is being ignored.

Once installed, you can run `tfsec` in the same directory as your Terraform configuration files. By default, TFSec will check all *.tf* files in the current directory and output any issues it finds, along with suggestions to fix them.

TFSec can be configured using a *.tfsec.yml* or *.tfsec.yaml* file to customize the scanner's behavior, ignore specific checks, or define custom checks. Like TFLint, consider integrating TFSec into your CI/CD pipeline or Git precommit hooks to automatically check your Terraform code for security issues before it's committed or deployed.

2.5 Validating Code with Preconditions and Postconditions

Problem

You want to validate your Terraform code by ensuring that specific conditions are met before applying the configuration (preconditions) and after applying the configuration (postconditions).

Solution

Utilize Terraform's variable validation and resource postconditions to enhance your Terraform code and module creation:

```
# Precondition: Variable validation
variable "instance_type" {
  type        = string
  description = "The instance type for the EC2 instance."

  validation {
    condition     = contains(["t2.micro", "t2.small"], var.instance_type)
    error_message = "The instance_type must be one of: t2.micro, t2.small."
  }
}

# Resource with postcondition
```

```
resource "aws_instance" "example" {
  ami           = "ami-0c947788c95c71c99"
  instance_type = var.instance_type

  tags = {
    Name = "example-instance"
  }

  # Postcondition
  lifecycle {
    postcondition {
      condition     = self.tags["Name"] == "example-instance"
      error_message = "The Name tag must be set to 'example-instance'."
    }
  }
}
```

Discussion

We define preconditions using the validation block within the variable block and postconditions using a null_resource with a local-exec provisioner.

The validation block allows you to specify a condition that must be true for the variable's value to be considered valid. In this example, we define a precondition that checks whether the value of the instance_type variable is one of the allowed values: "t2.micro", "t2.small", or "t2.medium". If the condition is not met, Terraform will display the specified error message and halt the execution.

Preconditions, implemented as variable validations, are checked before Terraform attempts to create or modify resources. They help ensure that input values are valid before any operations are performed. Postconditions, on the other hand, are checked after a resource has been created or updated. They verify that the resulting state of the resource meets specific criteria.

The postcondition is simulated using a null_resource with a local-exec provisioner that executes a shell command. In this case, the shell command uses the test command to verify the "Name" tag of the aws_instance.example resource is set to "example-instance." If the check fails, the shell command will return a nonzero exit code, and Terraform will report an error.

Use preconditions when you want to validate inputs before any resources are created or modified. This is particularly useful for catching configuration errors early. Use postconditions when you need to verify the state of a resource after it has been created or updated. This can help ensure the resource was configured correctly and met your requirements.

The local-exec provisioner is only used here for demonstration purposes to simulate postcondition checks. It's important to note that it executes locally on the machine running Terraform, and its use is unsuitable for most production use cases.

The `validation` block is available starting from Terraform 0.13, so make sure you are using a compatible version of Terraform.

In a real-world scenario, postconditions could be verified using external tools, scripts, or testing frameworks that can validate the state of the infrastructure and ensure it meets the expected criteria.

Please note that the `"ami"` value used in the `aws_instance` resource is just an example, and you should replace it with the appropriate AMI ID for your use case.

2.6 Validating Code with Open Policy Agent

Problem

You are developing Terraform configurations and want to ensure they comply with specific policies and best practices. To achieve this, you want to use Open Policy Agent (OPA) to validate your Terraform code against defined policies before applying the configuration. You need a solution to implement policy-as-code validation using OPA.

Solution

Dive deep into policy as code by defining a Terraform variable named `instance_type`, a foundational element for Open Policy Agent rules:

```
# terraform.rego
package terraform

# Define a policy to restrict allowed EC2 instance types
deny["Instance type must be t2.micro or t2.small"] {
  resource := input.resource_changes[_]
  resource.type == "aws_instance"
  instance_type := resource.change.after.instance_type
  not instance_type == "t2.micro"
  not instance_type == "t2.small"
}

# Define a policy to enforce tagging for EC2 instances
deny["All EC2 instances must have a Name tag"] {
  resource := input.resource_changes[_]
  resource.type == "aws_instance"
  tags := resource.change.after.tags
  not tags.Name
}

# Shell commands to run OPA evaluation
$ terraform init
$ terraform plan -out=tfplan
$ terraform show -json tfplan > tfplan.json
$ opa eval --data terraform.rego --input tfplan.json "data.terraform.deny"
```

Discussion

OPA is a general-purpose policy engine that allows you to define and enforce policies across your infrastructure. You can use OPA with Terraform to implement policy as code and validate your Terraform configurations against custom policies.

In this example, we defined two example policies in a Rego file named `terraform.rego`. The first policy restricts the allowed EC2 instance types to `"t2.micro"` and `"t2.small"`, while the second policy enforces that all EC2 instances must have a `Name` tag. The `deny` rules specify conditions under which a policy violation occurs.

The policy rules use the `input.resource_changes` array to represent the set of changes that Terraform plans to make. Each element in the array contains information about a planned change, including the type of resource, the change action (e.g., create, update, delete), and the before and after states of the resource.

Once the policies are defined, you can evaluate them against your Terraform plan using the `opa eval` command. To do this, you must generate a JSON representation of the Terraform plan using the `terraform show -json` command. The generated JSON file (`tfplan.json` in the example) is then provided as input to the `opa eval` command and the Rego policy file `terraform.rego`.

The `opa eval` command evaluates the policies against the Terraform plan and reports any policy violations. If there are no violations, the output will be empty. The output will show the messages defined in the `deny` rules if there are violations.

OPA provides a powerful way to enforce governance and compliance across your infrastructure code. It can be integrated into CI/CD pipelines to automate policy checks as part of the deployment process. To integrate OPA into your CI/CD pipeline, you can add a step that runs the OPA evaluation after the Terraform plan stage. If OPA reports any policy violations, the pipeline can be configured to fail, preventing noncompliant changes from being applied. Here's an example of how this might look in a GitHub Actions workflow:

```
- name: OPA Evaluation
  run: |
    terraform show -json tfplan > tfplan.json
    violations=$(opa eval --data terraform.rego --input tfplan.json "data.terraform.deny")
    if [ -n "$violations" ]; then
      echo "Policy violations found:"
      echo "$violations"
      exit 1
    fi
```

As your infrastructure evolves, remember to review and update your OPA policies regularly. This ensures that your policy checks remain relevant and continue to enforce your organization's latest standards and best practices.

2.7 Documenting Code with terraform-docs

Problem

You are developing Terraform modules and want to generate documentation automatically for your code. The documentation should include information about inputs, outputs, providers, and resources defined in the module. You need a solution to automate the generation of module documentation using the terraform-docs tool.

Solution

Strengthen your code documentation by leveraging terraform-docs, a unique approach for annotating your Terraform configuration:

```
# main.tf
provider "aws" {
  region = "us-west-2"
}

variable "instance_type" {
  type        = string
  description = "The instance type for the EC2 instance."
  default     = "t2.micro"
}

resource "aws_instance" "example" {
  ami           = "ami-0c947788c95c71c99" # Example Amazon Linux 2 AMI ID
  instance_type = var.instance_type

  tags = {
    Name = "example-instance"
  }
}

output "instance_public_ip" {
  value       = aws_instance.example.public_ip
  description = "The public IP address of the EC2 instance."
}

# Generate module documentation using terraform-docs
$ terraform-docs markdown ./ > README.md

# Generate module documentation in various formats
$ terraform-docs markdown table ./ > README.md
$ terraform-docs json ./ > docs.json
$ terraform-docs yaml ./ > docs.yaml
$ terraform-docs asciidoc table ./ > docs.adoc
```

Discussion

The terraform-docs tool is a third-party utility that automatically generates documentation for Terraform modules. It produces documentation based on the module's inputs, outputs, providers, resources, and other elements defined in the Terraform code. The tool can generate documentation in various formats, including Markdown, JSON, YAML, and HTML.

We provided an example Terraform module (`main.tf`) that includes a provider, variable, resource, and output. The module creates an AWS EC2 instance and exports the instance's public IP address as an output.

To generate documentation for this module, we used the `terraform-docs` command followed by the desired output format (`markdown`) and the path to the module directory (`./`). The generated documentation is then redirected to a file named *README.md* in the module directory. The *README.md* file will contain the generated documentation detailing the module's inputs, outputs, providers, and resources.

The `asciidoc` format is particularly useful for those who prefer AsciiDoc over Markdown for technical documentation. It offers more formatting options and is well suited for larger, more complex documentation needs.

It's important to note that `terraform-docs` uses the comments and descriptions in your Terraform code to generate the documentation. Therefore, providing meaningful descriptions for variables, outputs, and resources in your Terraform code is good practice to ensure the generated documentation is clear and informative.

`terraform-docs` allows for extensive customization of the output. You can create a *.terraform-docs.yml* file in your module directory to control which sections are included, how they're formatted, and more. For example:

```
formatter: markdown table

sections:
  show:
    - inputs
    - outputs
    - providers
    - requirements

sort:
  enabled: true
  by: required

settings:
  anchor: true
  color: true
  default: true
  escape: true
  indent: 2
  required: true
  sensitive: true
  type: true
```

Consider integrating `terraform-docs` into your Git precommit hooks or CI/CD pipeline to update documentation automatically when your Terraform code changes. This ensures your documentation stays up-to-date with your code.

2.8 Automating Code Validation with GitHub Actions

Problem

You want to automate the validation of your Terraform code whenever changes are pushed to your GitHub repository, ensuring that the code is valid before allowing it to be merged into the main branch.

Solution

Set the stage for automated code validation, where GitHub Actions workflows are often defined:

```
name: Terraform Validate

on:
  push:
    branches:
      - main
  pull_request:

jobs:
  validate:
    runs-on: ubuntu-latest
    steps:
      - name: Check out the repository
        uses: actions/checkout@v4

      - name: Set up Terraform
        uses: hashicorp/setup-terraform@v2
        with:
          terraform_version: 1.10.0

- name: Run tflint
        uses: terraform-linters/setup-tflint@v3
        with:
          tflint_version: v0.53.0  # Specify the version you want to use

      - name: Lint Terraform
        run: tflint --format=compact

- name: Run tfsec
        uses: aquasecurity/tfsec-action@v1.0.3
```

Discussion

The provided solution is a GitHub Actions workflow file named *terraform_validation.yml*, which should be placed in your GitHub repository's *.github/workflows* directory.

The workflow is triggered by push events to the `main` branch and all `pull_request` events. It defines a single job, `terraform_validation`, which runs on an `ubuntu-latest` virtual environment.

This GitHub Actions workflow automates several important checks:

1. It checks out your code and sets up Terraform.

2. It runs `terraform init` and `terraform validate` to catch basic syntax and configuration errors.

3. It uses `tflint` to catch stylistic issues and potential errors that `terraform validate` might miss.

4. It uses `tfsec` to identify potential security issues in your Terraform code.

5. By running these checks automatically on every push and pull request, you can catch and fix issues early in the development process before they make it into your main branch or production environment.

If the Terraform validation fails, the GitHub Actions workflow will show an error, preventing the changes from being merged until the issues are fixed. This ensures that only valid Terraform code is merged into the main branch.

You can further customize this workflow to fit your needs. For example, you might want to add steps to run `terraform plan` (using appropriate credentials) or to enforce a policy check using OPA, as discussed in previous sections.

2.9 Using Dependabot for Provider Version Updates

Problem

You want to automatically keep your Terraform provider versions up-to-date using GitHub's Dependabot, ensuring that your infrastructure code always uses the latest available features and bug fixes.

Solution

Prepare for a comprehensive process involving multiple steps aimed at configuring Dependabot for automated provider updates:

```
# .github/dependabot.yml
version: 2
updates:
  - package-ecosystem: "terraform"
    directory: "/"
    schedule:
      interval: "weekly"
    open-pull-requests-limit: 5
    allow:
      - dependency-type: "all"
    ignore:
      - dependency-name: "aws"
        versions: ["5.x"]  # Example: ignore major version upgrades
```

Discussion

The provided solution is a Dependabot configuration file named *dependabot.yml*, which should be placed in the *.github* directory of your GitHub repository.

Let's break down the configuration:

`package-ecosystem`
Set to `"terraform"` to update Terraform providers and modules.

`directory`
The `"/"` indicates Dependabot should check the root directory of your repository.

`schedule`
Set to check weekly. You can adjust this based on your needs.

`open-pull-requests-limit`
Limits the number of open pull requests Dependabot can have simultaneously.

`allow`
Specifies which dependencies can be updated. `"all"` includes direct and indirect dependencies.

`ignore`
Allows you to exclude specific updates. In this example, we're ignoring major version upgrades for the AWS provider.

With this configuration in place, Dependabot will automatically check for updates to your Terraform providers daily, create pull requests with the updates, and target the main branch. This helps ensure that your infrastructure code remains up-to-date and secure.

When Dependabot opens a pull request to update a provider, make sure to:

1. Review the changelog for the new version to understand what's changed.

2. Run your Terraform validation and automated tests against the updated version.

3. Consider any potential breaking changes and how they might affect your infrastructure.

4. Update your code if necessary to accommodate any changes in the provider.

Regularly updating your providers is crucial for security. Providers often include patches for vulnerabilities, so keeping them up-to-date helps maintain the security of your infrastructure. However, always test thoroughly before applying updates to production environments.

2.10 Using GitHub Codespaces and DevContainers

Problem

You want to set up a consistent development environment for your Terraform project using GitHub Codespaces and DevContainers, ensuring all contributors have the same toolset and dependencies.

Solution

Getting this recipe working contains several steps, so buckle up and prepare for all these moving parts. We'll be using GitHub (*https://github.com*), VS Code (*https://oreil.ly/iGimw*), and a browser to complete these steps, so be sure to sign up and download those as you need.

To begin, create a *.devcontainer* folder at the root of your directory, then an empty *Dockerfile* and *devcontainer.json* file (see Figure 2-1).

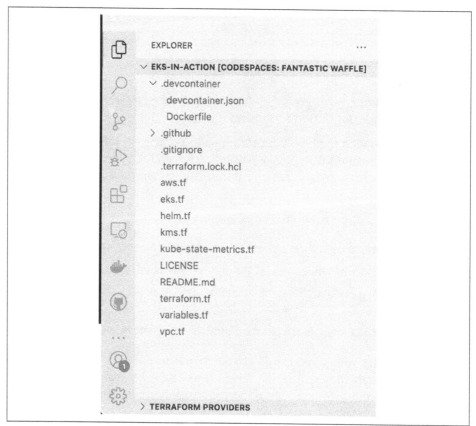

Figure 2-1. When viewing your files in VS Code, you should see this

We'll start by editing the *Dockerfile* and adding key configuration lines:

```
FROM hashicorp/terraform:latest

RUN apt-get update && apt-get install -y git
```

Next, with the following lines, we specify the JSON configuration for how our codespace container will work in the *devcontainer.json* file:

```
{
  "name": "Terraform Development Container",
  "build": {
    "dockerfile": "Dockerfile"
  },
  "extensions": [
    "hashicorp.terraform",
    "ms-azuretools.vscode-docker"
  ],
  "settings": {
    "terminal.integrated.shell.linux": "/bin/bash"
  }
}
```

Now, commit and push your changes to the repository you're working with on GitHub.

> Ensure your changes are pushed to GitHub, or these next steps will not work.

Once your code is on GitHub, you will notice that you have unlocked a new capability, Codespaces. To create your codespace, you can use the button within the GitHub UI (see Figure 2-2), or you can try some of the other creation options (*https://oreil.ly/zW_xP*).

The first time you load your codespace, it may take a few moments to build and load within your browser or VS Code.

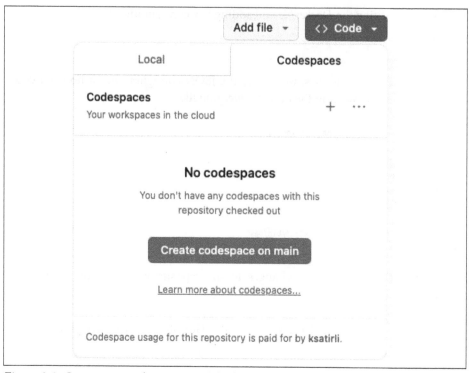

Figure 2-2. Create your codespace using the button within the GitHub UI

Once the codespace has loaded, you will see something resembling Figure 2-3 in your browser (or within VS Code).

As a final step, you can run `terraform version` in the terminal window of your codespace and confirm that you can use Terraform in the cloud.

Figure 2-3. Resulting page after the Codespace has loaded

Discussion

This setup provides a consistent environment with Terraform preinstalled and helpful VS Code extensions. It ensures all team members work with the same tools and versions, reducing "works on my machine" issues. Remember to secure any credentials or sensitive information when using cloud-based development environments. Consider using environment variables or integrating them with a secure secret management system to handle cloud provider credentials.

We first created a metadata folder that houses configuration information that installs the Terraform binary and links together in a place where we can work with our IaC, plan, validate, apply, and perform edits in real time. This example shows the minimal configuration required to run this codespace. However, you can edit this for any workflow you can imagine or install any other binaries or tools needed.

While codespaces offers a convenient solution, there are other ways to achieve consistent development environments, such as using local containers with VS Code's Remote-Containers extension or other cloud-based IDE solutions. Choose the approach that best fits your team's needs and security requirements.

2.11 Limiting Blast Radius with Terraform

Problem

You want to minimize the potential impact of changes in your Terraform-managed infrastructure, ensuring that modifications in one area don't unintentionally affect others.

Solution

Implement the following practices to limit the blast radius of your Terraform operations:

1. Modularize your code:

```
# main.tf
module "networking" {
  source = "./modules/networking"
  # ... module parameters ...
}

module "compute" {
  source = "./modules/compute"
  # ... module parameters ...
}
```

2. Use HCP Terraform for state management:

```
terraform {
  cloud {
    organization = "your-org-name"

    workspaces {
      name = "your-workspace-name"
    }
  }
}
```

3. Implement fine-grained IAM policies:

```
resource "aws_iam_role" "example" {
  name = "limited-s3-access"

  assume_role_policy = jsonencode({
    Version = "2012-10-17"
    Statement = [
      {
        Action = "sts:AssumeRole"
        Effect = "Allow"
        Principal = {
          Service = "ec2.amazonaws.com"
        }
      }
    ]
  })
}

resource "aws_iam_role_policy_attachment" "example" {
```

```
    role       = aws_iam_role.example.name
    policy_arn = "arn:aws:iam::aws:policy/AmazonS3ReadOnlyAccess"
}
```

4. Use variables to control resource creation:

```
variable "enable_feature_x" {
  type        = bool
  default     = false
  description = "Whether to enable Feature X resources"
}

resource "aws_instance" "feature_x" {
  count = var.enable_feature_x ? 1 : 0
  # ... instance configuration ...
}
```

Discussion

Limiting the blast radius in Terraform involves several best practices:

Modularize your code
Breaking your infrastructure into smaller, reusable modules allows you to independently isolate changes and manage components. This makes it easier to understand the impact of changes and reduces the risk of unintended side effects.

Use HCP Terraform for state management
HCP Terraform provides a secure, centralized location for managing state files. Using separate workspaces for different environments (dev, staging, prod) ensures that changes in one environment don't affect others. This approach also offers benefits such as state locking to prevent concurrent modifications and role-based access control for team collaboration.

Implement fine-grained IAM policies
Follow the principle of least privilege when defining IAM roles and policies. In this example, we created a role that only allows read access to S3. This limits the potential damage caused by a misconfiguration or compromise.

Use variables to control resource creation
You can easily limit the scope of changes by using variables to toggle the creation of resources or entire feature sets. This is particularly useful for testing new features or managing different configurations across environments.

Implement strong change management practices
Use Git branches, pull requests, and code reviews to ensure changes are thoroughly vetted before being applied. Consider using Terraform's plan output as part of your review process to understand the changes that will be made.

Leverage HCP Terraform's sentinel policies
Use sentinel policies to enforce governance rules across your infrastructure. This can prevent noncompliant resources from being created or modified.

Use smaller, more frequent applies

Instead of making significant, sweeping changes, aim for smaller, incremental updates. This makes it easier to identify and roll back problematic changes.

Regularly test your infrastructure code

Implement unit tests for your modules and integration tests for your complete setup. Tools such as Terratest can be valuable for this purpose.

Use Terraform's `-target` flag judiciously

While not recommended for regular use, the `-target` flag can help limit the scope of an apply operation during troubleshooting or emergencies.

By implementing these practices, you can significantly reduce the risk of unintended changes and limit the impact of any issues. Remember, the goal is to create an infrastructure that is not only efficient but also resilient and manageable.

## CHAPTER 3

Terraform Syntax Patterns

Terraform functions give users the flexibility and power to manipulate data within their configuration files. They facilitate data transformation, perform arithmetic, and aid in working with complex data types such as lists, maps, and objects. They allow users to construct more dynamic and adaptable Terraform configurations at their core.

3.1 Cleaning User Inputs with trimspace

Problem

While creating infrastructure using Terraform, user inputs often need to be processed for extra whitespace, newlines, or other unexpected characters. This can lead to errors or inconsistencies in resource creation if not correctly handled. Therefore, knowing how to clean user inputs using Terraform's built-in functions like chomp and trimspace is essential.

Solution

Establish a robust foundation for input sanitization by introducing a dedicated variable, which will be the target for applying the trimspace function:

```
variable "user_input" {
  description = "The user input that needs cleaning"
  type = string
  default = " \nExample user input with leading and trailing spaces\n "
}

locals {
  clean_user_input = trimspace(var.user_input)
}

output "clean_user_input" {
```

```
  value = local.clean_user_input
}
```

Discussion

In this code snippet, we are declaring a variable named `user_input`. This will serve as our raw, unprocessed input from the user. It's set with a default value that includes leading and trailing whitespace and newlines for demonstration.

Next, we define a local value named `clean_user_input` using Terraform's built-in `chomp` and `trimspace` functions. These functions will clean the user input. `trimspace` is a function that takes a string argument and returns a copy of the string with all spaces removed from the start and end of the string. This does not affect spaces elsewhere in the string.

On the other hand, the `chomp` function removes newline characters at the end of a string. This is useful for file reading functions where you just want to read the content, not newlines.

When used in the order `trimspace(var.user_input)`, this function will remove any leading or trailing spaces and newline characters from the user input.

Finally, an output is defined that displays the cleaned user input. You can see the results by running `terraform apply`, showing you the cleaned string without leading or trailing whitespaces or newline characters.

3.2 Removing Prefixes and Suffixes

Problem

In specific scenarios, you might receive user inputs or outputs from other resources with known prefixes or suffixes that need removal before further use. Terraform does not have a built-in function to directly remove prefixes or suffixes from strings, so we need a workaround to accomplish this.

Solution

Initiate your exploration of string manipulation by defining a Terraform variable named `user_input`, setting the stage for prefix and suffix removal techniques:

```
variable "user_input" {
  description = "The user input that needs cleaning"
  type        = string
  default     = "prefix_exampleUserInput_suffix"
}

locals {
  prefix = "prefix_"
  suffix = "_suffix"
```

```
  without_prefix   = trimprefix(var.user_input, local.prefix)
  clean_user_input = trimsuffix(local.without_prefix, local.suffix)
}

output "clean_user_input" {
  value = local.clean_user_input
}
```

Discussion

In the given HCL code, a variable `user_input` is created to represent the user input. It's set with a default value that includes a prefix and a suffix for demonstration purposes.

Next, we define two locals, `prefix` and `suffix`, to represent the strings that must be removed from the user input.

The `replace` function in Terraform takes three arguments:

- The input string
- The search string
- The replacement string

Here, we use nested `replace` function calls to remove prefixes and suffixes. We are replacing the prefix and suffix in the user input with an empty string ("").

Finally, we define an output named `clean_user_input`, which outputs the processed string after removing the prefix and suffix. Running `terraform apply` will show you the cleaned string without the prefix and suffix.

3.3 Working with Regular Expressions

Problem

In certain situations, while handling user input or transforming strings in Terraform, you should use regular expressions (regex). Terraform supports several regex functions like `regex`, `regexall`, and `replace`. The problem is understanding how to effectively use these regular expressions in your Terraform scripts.

Solution

Delve into the world of regular expressions by configuring a variable called `user_input`, a critical first step for pattern matching:

```
variable "user_input" {
  description = "The user input that needs processing"
  type        = string
```

```
  default    = "123-45-6789"
}

locals {
  masked_input = replace(var.user_input,
    regex("\\d{3}-\\d{2}-(\\d{4})", var.user_input),
    "XXX-XX-$1"
  )
}

output "masked_input" {
  value = local.masked_input
}
```

Discussion

This HCL code demonstrates regular expressions with the replace function in Terraform. We first declare a variable user_input, a string resembling a Social Security number (SSN). This variable is used to demonstrate the replacement operation.

We define a local value masked_input where we use the replace function. This function typically replaces a substring with another substring in a given string, but it also supports regex.

In this example, the replace function is used with a regex pattern that matches the format of an SSN (i.e., XXX-XX-XXXX). The pattern \\d{3}-\\d{2}-(\\d{4}) captures three digits followed by a hyphen, two digits followed by a hyphen, and finally, four digits.

The parentheses around \\d{4} capture the last four digits so we can use them in the replacement string. The double backslashes are needed to escape the backslash in the Terraform string.

In the replacement string "XXX-XX-\1", \1 refers to the first captured group in the regex (in this case, the last four digits of the SSN).

Finally, an output named masked_input is declared to print the transformed string after running terraform apply. This output will show the SSN in a masked format, with only the last four digits visible.

Terraform provides several functions for working with regular expressions:

regex
: Applies a regular expression to a string and returns the matching substrings

regexall
: Similar to regex, but returns all matches, not just the first

replace
: Replaces substrings in a given string using a regular expression

The `replace` function in Terraform performs a global replacement by default, which replaces all occurrences of the pattern in the string. It doesn't have built-in support for lazy matching or replacement, only the last occurrence.

In our example, we use `regex` within `replace` to capture the last four digits of the social security number and preserve them in the masked output. The `$1` in the replacement string refers to the first captured group (the last four digits).

If you need more complex regex operations, such as replacing only the last occurrence or using lazy matching, you might need to use multiple regex operations or consider preprocessing your data before passing it to Terraform.

Remember that while `regex` is powerful, complex operations can make your Terraform code harder to read and maintain. Use them judiciously and consider adding comments to explain nontrivial regex patterns.

3.4 Advanced String Manipulation

Problem

Sometimes, you must perform multiple string replacements or transformations in a single operation. This can be particularly useful when standardizing input data or applying multiple formatting rules to a string.

Solution

Use nested `replace` functions or the `format` function in combination with `replace` to perform multiple string manipulations in one step:

```
variable "user_input" {
  description = "The user input that needs processing"
  type        = string
  default     = "hello, world! 123"
}

locals {
  processed_input = replace(
    replace(
      upper(var.user_input),
      "WORLD",
      "TERRAFORM"
    ),
    "!",
    "!!!"
  )
}

output "processed_input" {
  value = local.processed_input
}
```

Discussion

In this example, we perform multiple string manipulations on the input:

1. Convert the entire string to uppercase using the upper function.

2. Replace "WORLD" with "TERRAFORM" using the replace function.

3. Replace "!" with "!!!" using another replace function.

This demonstrates how you can chain multiple string manipulation functions to achieve complex transformations in a single operation.

For even more complex scenarios, you might consider using the format function in combination with replace:

```
locals {
  complex_transformation = format(
    "%s: %s",
    upper(replace(var.user_input, "hello", "greetings")),
    replace(var.user_input, "\\d+", "NumbersRemoved")
  )
}
```

This example replaces "hello" with "greetings" and converts the result to upper-case for the first part of the output. For the second part, it removes all numbers from the input string. The format function then combines these two transformed parts into a single string.

Remember that while these nested functions are powerful, they can become difficult to read if overused. Consider breaking down complex transformations into multiple steps with intermediate variables for better readability and maintainability.

3.5 Working with Case-Sensitive Strings Using title, upper, and lower

Problem

In Terraform configurations, you often need to standardize the case of string inputs or generate outputs with specific capitalization. This is common when working with naming conventions or preparing data for external systems with case-sensitive requirements.

Solution

Terraform provides three built-in functions for case transformation: title(), upper(), and lower(). Use these functions to convert strings to title case, uppercase, or lowercase, respectively:

```
variable "input_string" {
  description = "The string to be case-transformed"
  type        = string
  default     = "hello, WORLD! This is TerraForm."
}

locals {
  title_case = title(var.input_string)
  upper_case = upper(var.input_string)
  lower_case = lower(var.input_string)
}

output "case_transformations" {
  value = {
    original   = var.input_string
    title_case = local.title_case
    upper_case = local.upper_case
    lower_case = local.lower_case
  }
}
```

Discussion

In this example, we demonstrate the use of all three case transformation functions:

title()
>   Converts the first character of each word to uppercase and the rest to lowercase

upper()
>   Converts all characters in the string to uppercase

lower()
>   Converts all characters in the string to lowercase

Applying this configuration lets you see how each function affects the input string differently.

It's important to note that these functions are designed primarily for use with English text and may not handle special cases or non-Latin scripts correctly. For example:

- The title() function may not correctly capitalize words such as "McDonalds" or "iPhone."

- These functions may not work as expected with languages that don't use letter case (e.g., Chinese, Japanese) or have different case rules (e.g., German "ß").

For more complex internationalization needs, you should preprocess your strings before passing them to Terraform or handle case transformations in a different layer of your application.

Additionally, be aware that case transformations are not always reversible. For instance, if you apply lower() and title() to a string, you may not return to the original capitalization.

Use these functions to ensure consistent formatting of strings within your Terraform configurations, especially for resource naming or when interfacing with case-sensitive external systems. However, the limitations and potential edge cases when working with diverse text inputs should be considered.

3.6 Alphabetically Sorting Lists

Problem

When working with lists in Terraform, you often need to sort the elements for consistency and readability or to meet specific requirements of external systems or policies.

Solution

Use Terraform's built-in sort function to sort a list of strings alphabetically:

```
variable "unsorted_list" {
  description = "List of strings to be sorted"
  type        = list(string)
  default     = ["banana", "apple", "cherry", "date", "elderberry"]
}

locals {
  sorted_list = sort(var.unsorted_list)
}

output "sorted_output" {
  value = local.sorted_list
}
```

Discussion

The sort function in Terraform takes a list of strings and returns a new list with those strings sorted in lexicographic order (alphabetical order based on UTF-8 values). Here's what you need to know:

Behavior
The sort is ascending and case-sensitive. Uppercase letters come before lowercase letters.

Data types
sort only works with lists of strings. For lists of numbers or other data types, you'll need to convert to strings first or use a different approach.

Limitations

Problems with sorting:

- It doesn't support custom sorting rules or locales.
- It may not sort non-Latin scripts or accented characters as expected.
- It doesn't provide options for descending order or case-insensitive sorting.

Use cases

Sorting is helpful for:

- Ensuring consistent ordering in output or resource names
- Meeting requirements of systems that expect sorted input
- Improving the readability of configuration or output

Performance

For most use cases in Terraform, the performance impact of sorting is negligible. However, for very large lists, consider whether sorting is necessary.

When using sorted lists to deploy infrastructure, be cautious about the potential implications:

```
resource "example_resource" "sorted_deployment" {
  count = length(var.unsorted_list)
  name  = sort(var.unsorted_list)[count.index]
}
```

In this scenario, changing the input list could result in resources being renamed or re-created, potentially causing unintended disruptions. Always consider the impact of sorting on your specific use case.

For more complex sorting needs, such as custom ordering or sorting by multiple criteria, you might need to preprocess your data before passing it to Terraform or handle the sorting in a different layer of your application.

3.7 Creating Subnets from a CIDR Block

Problem

When designing network infrastructure in cloud environments, you often must divide a large CIDR block into smaller subnets. This task requires precise calculations to ensure proper network segmentation. When designing network infrastructure, it's crucial to understand how CIDR blocks are divided into subnets. This process involves precise calculations to ensure proper network segmentation. Figure 3-1 illustrates this concept visually.

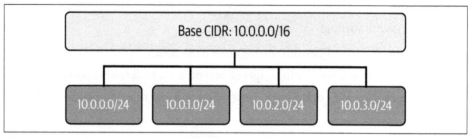

Figure 3-1. Creating subnets from a CIDR block

Solution

Use Terraform's `cidrsubnet` function to calculate subnet CIDR blocks from a larger CIDR block automatically:

```
locals {
  base_cidr_block = "10.0.0.0/16"

  # Create four /24 subnets
  subnets = [for i in range(4) : cidrsubnet(local.base_cidr_block, 8, i)]
}

output "subnet_cidr_blocks" {
  value = local.subnets
}
```

Discussion

The `cidrsubnet` function in Terraform is a powerful tool for network address planning. Here's a breakdown of how it works:

- Function signature: `cidrsubnet(prefix, newbits, netnum)`
  - `prefix`: The starting CIDR block
  - `newbits`: Number of additional bits with which to extend the prefix
  - `netnum`: The number that will be used to generate the new subnet
- In our example:
  - We start with a /16 CIDR block (65,536 IP addresses).
  - We add 8 bits (newbits) to create /24 `subnets` (256 IP addresses each).
  - We generate four subnets using a `for` loop and the `range` function.
- The result will be four /24 subnets: `"10.0.0.0/24"`, `"10.0.1.0/24"`, `"10.0.2.0/24"`, and `"10.0.3.0/24"`.

This approach offers several advantages:

Automation
    It eliminates manual subnet calculations, reducing errors.

Scalability
    You can easily adjust the number of subnets by changing the loop.

Flexibility
    By modifying the `newbits` parameter, you can create different-sized subnets.

However, be aware of some considerations:

Subnet size
    Ensure your chosen subnet size can accommodate your expected number of IP addresses.

IP address waste
    Creating too many small subnets can lead to inefficient IP address usage.

Cloud provider limits
    Some providers have limits on the number of subnets per VPC.

Combine `cidrsubnet` with other functions like `cidrhost` to assign specific IP addresses within your subnets for more complex network designs:

```
locals {
  first_ip_in_each_subnet = [for subnet in local.subnets : cidrhost(subnet, 1)]
}
```

This example finds the first usable IP address in each subnet, which could be useful for assigning gateway IP addresses or other fixed network resources.

Using `cidrsubnet` and related functions, you can create flexible, scalable network configurations in your Terraform code, ensuring consistent and error-free subnet allocation across your infrastructure.

3.8 Interacting with the Local Filesystem

Problem

Terraform configurations sometimes need to read from or check the existence of local files, such as when importing external data or verifying prerequisites.

Solution

Use Terraform's `file` and `fileexists` functions to interact with the local filesystem. Here's an example:

```
variable "config_file_path" {
  description = "Path to the configuration file"
  type        = string
  default     = "config.txt"
}

locals {
  file_content = fileexists(var.config_file_path) ? file(var.config_file_path) : "Default content"
}

output "file_content" {
  value = local.file_content
}
```

Discussion

This example demonstrates two key functions for filesystem interaction:

`fileexists(path)`
> Returns `true` if a file exists at the given path

`file(path)`
> Reads the contents of the file at the given path

By combining these functions, we can create more robust configurations:

- We use a variable for the `file` path, allowing flexibility and reusability.
- The `fileexists` check prevents errors if the file is missing.
- We provide a default value if the file doesn't exist.

Here are some important considerations when working with local files in Terraform:

Relative paths
> Paths are relative to the directory where Terraform is run, not necessarily where the *.tf* file is located.

Security
> Be cautious about reading sensitive data from files. Consider using Terraform's secret management features for sensitive information.

Portability
> Configurations that depend on local files may be less portable across different environments.

Be mindful of how you manage files that your Terraform configuration depends on in your version control system.

File changes
Terraform doesn't automatically detect changes to external files. You may need to use the `-replaceflag` or `terraform taint` to force resource updates.

Here's an advanced example that reads multiple files:

```
variable "config_files" {
  description = "List of configuration file paths"
  type        = list(string)
  default     = ["config1.txt", "config2.txt", "config3.txt"]
}

locals {
  config_contents = {
    for path in var.config_files :
    path => fileexists(path) ? file(path) : "File not found: ${path}"
  }
}

output "configurations" {
  value = local.config_contents
}
```

This script reads multiple configuration files and maps their contents, handling missing files gracefully.

Remember, while these functions are helpful, they should be used judiciously. Excessive reliance on local files can make your Terraform configurations less portable and more challenging to manage in team environments. You can use Terraform's native constructs, such as variables, data sources, and remote states, to share information between different configuration parts.

3.9 Rendering Templates

Problem

You must generate configuration files or scripts based on variable inputs in Terraform. This is where templates come into play. Terraform provides a powerful templating language to help render templates based on your inputs. Rendering templates is a powerful technique in Terraform for generating configuration files or scripts dynamically based on input variables. Figure 3-2 provides a visual representation of how this process works in the context of IaC.

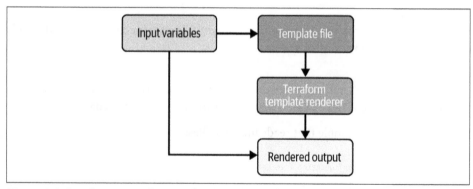

Figure 3-2. Rendering templates with IaC

Solution

Prepare to dynamically generate configuration files by reading data from a file, a preliminary step for template rendering:

```
variable "user_name" {
  description = "User name for the script"
  type        = string
  default     = "Taylor"
}

data "template_file" "bash_script" {
  template = <<-EOF
           #!/bin/bash
           echo "Hello, ${user_name}"
           EOF

  vars = {
    user_name = var.user_name
  }
}

output "rendered_script" {
  description = "Rendered bash script"
  value       = data.template_file.bash_script.rendered
}
```

Discussion

In this HCL code, we first declare a variable user_name, which will be used as a variable input in our template.

We then define a template_file data source named bash_script. This is where we specify our template content and the variables that we will use in the template.

We use the "heredoc" syntax in the template attribute to specify a multiline string that represents our bash script. Within this template, we use ${user_name} to interpolate the value of the user_name variable.

In the template language, ${...} is used for interpolation, similar to HCL, but you must use double dollar signs ($${...}) if you want to produce an actual dollar sign followed by a brace in the rendered output.

The vars block contains the actual values for each variable in our template. In this case, we set user_name to the value of the user_name variable declared at the top of our script.

Finally, we declare an output rendered_script that will print the rendered script after running terraform apply. This output will contain the actual content of the bash script with ${user_name} replaced with the value from the user_name variable.

Rendering templates helps generate configuration files or scripts based on variable inputs. This allows you to create flexible and reusable code.

3.10 Validating Input Strings

Problem

When accepting input variables in Terraform, you often need to ensure that the values meet certain criteria to prevent configuration errors or security issues.

Solution

Use Terraform's variable block with a validation rule to enforce constraints on input values. Here's an example:

```
variable "environment" {
  type        = string
  description = "The deployment environment (dev, staging, or prod)"

  validation {
    condition     = contains(["dev", "staging", "prod"], var.environment)
    error_message = "The environment must be dev, staging, or prod."
  }
}

variable "instance_count" {
  type        = number
  description = "Number of instances to create"

  validation {
    condition     = var.instance_count > 0 && var.instance_count <= 10
    error_message = "Instance count must be between 1 and 10."
  }
}
```

Discussion

Terraform's variable validation feature allows you to define rules that input values must satisfy.

Here's how it works:

1. The `validation` block is added within a variable block.

2. The `condition` attribute contains an expression that must evaluate to `true` for the input to be valid.

3. The `error_message` is displayed if the condition is not met.

Key points to remember:

Multiple validations

You can have multiple `validation` blocks for a single variable to check different conditions.

Complex conditions

The condition can use any Terraform functions or operators, allowing for sophisticated validation logic.

Custom error messages

Craft clear error messages to help users understand why their input was rejected.

Validation timing

Validation occurs when Terraform loads the configuration and when applying changes, not just at apply time.

Type constraints

The `type` argument provides basic type checking. Use `validation` for more specific rules within a type.

Here's an advanced example with multiple validations:

```
variable "vpc_cidr" {
  type        = string
  description = "CIDR block for the VPC"

  validation {
    condition     = can(cidrhost(var.vpc_cidr, 0))
    error_message = "Must be a valid IPv4 CIDR block."
  }

  validation {
    condition     = split("/", var.vpc_cidr)[1] <= "24" && split("/", var.vpc_cidr)[1] >= "16"
    error_message = "VPC CIDR block must be between a /16 and /24."
  }
}
```

This example validates that the input is both a valid CIDR block and within an acceptable size range.

 Important note on complex validations: For highly complex validations, especially those involving pattern matching (e.g., email addresses), be cautious about relying solely on Terraform's validation capabilities. Complex regex patterns can be difficult to maintain and may not cover all edge cases. For such scenarios, consider:

- Using external data sources or scripts for validation
- Implementing validation logic in your deployment pipeline outside of Terraform
- Using specialized libraries or services for complex validations, such as email addresses

Remember, while input validation is crucial for creating robust Terraform configurations, balancing thoroughness with maintainability and user experience is important.

3.11 Optimistically Retrieving Data Using can and try

Problem

When working with complex data structures or external data sources in Terraform, you may encounter situations where certain values might be missing or in an unexpected format. This can lead to errors if not handled properly.

Solution

Use Terraform's `can` and `try` functions to handle potential errors gracefully and provide default values when necessary. Here's an example using security group rules:

```
variable "security_rules" {
  type = map(object({
    type        = string
    from_port   = number
    to_port     = number
    protocol    = string
    cidr_blocks = list(string)
  }))
  default = {
    http = {
      type        = "ingress"
      from_port   = 80
      to_port     = 80
      protocol    = "tcp"
      cidr_blocks = ["0.0.0.0/0"]
    },
    https = {
      type        = "ingress"
      from_port   = 443
```

```
      to_port    = 443
      protocol   = "tcp"
      cidr_blocks = ["0.0.0.0/0"]
    }
  }
}

resource "aws_security_group" "example" {
  name        = "example"
  description = "Example security group"

  dynamic "ingress" {
    for_each = var.security_rules
    content {
      type        = try(ingress.value.type, "ingress")
      from_port   = ingress.value.from_port
      to_port     = ingress.value.to_port
      protocol    = ingress.value.protocol
      cidr_blocks = can(ingress.value.cidr_blocks) ? ingress.value.cidr_blocks : null
    }
  }
}
```

Discussion

The `can` and `try` functions in Terraform help you write more resilient code by handling potential errors gracefully:

`can(expression)`
> Returns `true` if the expression can be evaluated without error, and `false` otherwise

`try(expression, fallback_value)`
> Attempts to evaluate the expression, returning the `fallback` value if an error occurs

In our example:

- We use `try` to provide a default value for the `type` attribute. If `ingress.value.type` is missing or invalid, it defaults to `"ingress"`.

- We use `can` to check if `cidr_blocks` exists and is valid. If not, we set it to `null`, which AWS interprets as "allow all."

Key points to remember:

Error suppression
> While `can` and `try` are useful, be cautious not to suppress important errors that should be addressed.

Default values
> When using `try`, choose sensible default values that won't introduce security risks or unexpected behavior.

Readability

Overuse of `can` and `try` can make your code harder to read, so use them judiciously.

Debugging

These functions can make it harder to debug issues, as they suppress errors that might be important.

Here's an advanced example that processes a map of security rules with optional attributes:

```
variable "advanced_security_rules" {
  type = map(object({
    type        = optional(string)
    from_port   = number
    to_port     = number
    protocol    = string
    cidr_blocks = optional(list(string))
    description = optional(string)
  }))
  default = {
    http = {
      from_port = 80
      to_port   = 80
      protocol  = "tcp"
    },
    https = {
      from_port   = 443
      to_port     = 443
      protocol    = "tcp"
      description = "HTTPS traffic"
    }
  }
}

locals {
  processed_rules = {
    for key, rule in var.advanced_security_rules :
    key => {
      type        = try(rule.type, "ingress")
      from_port   = rule.from_port
      to_port     = rule.to_port
      protocol    = rule.protocol
      cidr_blocks = can(rule.cidr_blocks) ? rule.cidr_blocks : ["0.0.0.0/0"]
      description = try(rule.description, "Managed by Terraform")
    }
  }
}
```

This example demonstrates how to process a map of security rules, providing default values for optional attributes using `can` and `try`.

Remember, while `can` and `try` are powerful tools for handling potential errors, they should be used thoughtfully. Always consider whether it's better to explicitly handle an error or allow Terraform to fail fast when unexpected conditions occur.

3.12 Sequentially Processing Input Data

Problem

In Terraform, you sometimes need to process a list of input data in a specific order, particularly when creating resources that have dependencies based on their position in a sequence. Sequential processing of input data is sometimes necessary in Terraform, especially when dealing with resources that have dependencies based on their position in a sequence. Figure 3-3 illustrates this concept, showing how data flows through the sequential processing steps.

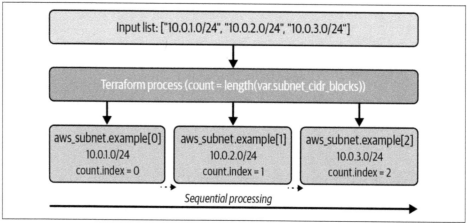

Figure 3-3. Sequentially processing input data

Solution

Use Terraform's for expressions in combination with the index function to process list items sequentially. Here's an example:

```
variable "subnet_cidr_blocks" {
  type    = list(string)
  default = ["10.0.1.0/24", "10.0.2.0/24", "10.0.3.0/24"]
}

resource "aws_subnet" "example" {
  count             = length(var.subnet_cidr_blocks)
  vpc_id            = aws_vpc.main.id
  cidr_block        = var.subnet_cidr_blocks[count.index]
  availability_zone = data.aws_availability_zones.available.names[count.index % length
    (data.aws_availability_zones.available.names)]

  tags = {
    Name = "Subnet-${count.index + 1}"
  }
}
```

Discussion

While Terraform is primarily declarative and often processes resources in parallel, there are scenarios where sequential processing is necessary or beneficial. Here's how the example works:

- We use the `count` meta-argument to create multiple subnet resources based on the length of our CIDR block list.
- The `count.index` allows us to access the current iteration index, ensuring we use the correct CIDR block for each subnet.
- We use the modulo operator (%) to cycle through available availability zones, distributing subnets across them sequentially.

Key points to remember:

Order preservation
Terraform generally maintains the order of list elements, but it's not guaranteed in all contexts.

Resource dependencies
Resources created this way will have implicit dependencies based on their index. For example, `aws_subnet.example` depends on `aws_subnet.example`.

Updates and deletions
Be cautious when adding or removing elements from the middle of the input list, as it can cause resources to be re-created or deleted.

Scalability
This approach works well for small- to medium-sized lists but may become unwieldy for very large lists.

Here's an advanced example that demonstrates sequential processing with interdependent resources:

```
variable "app_names" {
  type    = list(string)
  default = ["app1", "app2", "app3"]
}

resource "aws_iam_role" "example" {
  count = length(var.app_names)
  name  = "role-${var.app_names[count.index]}"

  assume_role_policy = jsonencode({
    Version = "2012-10-17"
    Statement = [
      {
        Action = "sts:AssumeRole"
        Effect = "Allow"
        Principal = {
          Service = "ec2.amazonaws.com"
```

```
      }
    }
  ]
})
}

resource "aws_iam_instance_profile" "example" {
  count = length(var.app_names)
  name  = "profile-${var.app_names[count.index]}"
  role  = aws_iam_role.example[count.index].name
}

resource "aws_instance" "example" {
  count                  = length(var.app_names)
  ami                    = data.aws_ami.example.id
  instance_type          = "t2.micro"
  iam_instance_profile   = aws_iam_instance_profile.example[count.index].name
  vpc_security_group_ids = [aws_security_group.example.id]

  tags = {
    Name = var.app_names[count.index]
  }

  depends_on = [aws_iam_role.example]
}
```

This example creates a series of identity and access management (IAM) roles, instance profiles, and EC2 instances, ensuring each instance is associated with its corresponding role and profile.

Remember, while this approach allows for sequential processing, Terraform's strength lies in its declarative management of resources. When possible, design your configurations to be order independent to take full advantage of Terraform's parallel execution capabilities.

3.13 Good Error Messages for Bad Input

Problem

When users provide invalid inputs to your Terraform module, generic error messages can be confusing and unhelpful. You need a way to provide clear, specific feedback about what went wrong and how to fix it.

Solution

Use Terraform's variable block with custom validation rules to create informative error messages for invalid inputs. Here's an example:

```
variable "instance_type" {
  type        = string
  description = "The EC2 instance type"

  validation {
    condition     = can(regex("^t[23]\\..*", var.instance_type))
    error_message = "Invalid instance
```

```
        type. Must be a t2 or t3 instance type (e.g., t2.micro, t3.small)."
  }
}

variable "environment" {
  type        = string
  description = "The deployment environment"

  validation {
    condition     = contains(["dev", "staging", "prod"], var.environment)
    error_message = "Invalid environment. Must be one of: dev, staging, prod."
  }
}

variable "db_settings" {
  type = object({
    instance_class = string
    storage_type   = string
    storage_size   = number
  })

  validation {
    condition     = can(regex("^db\\.[tmrc][3-6]\\..*", var.db_settings.instance_class))
    error_message = "Invalid DB instance class. Must be a valid RDS instance type
      (e.g., db.t3.micro, db.m5.large)."
  }

  validation {
    condition     = contains(["gp2", "io1"], var.db_settings.storage_type)
    error_message = "Invalid storage type. Must be either 'gp2' or 'io1'. For high-performance
      requirements, use 'io1'."
  }

  validation {
    condition     = var.db_settings.storage_size >= 20 && var.db_settings.storage_size <= 65536
    error_message = "Invalid storage size. Must be between 20 GiB and 65,536 GiB. For larger sizes,
      consider using a larger instance class."
  }
}
```

Discussion

Crafting good error messages is crucial for improving the usability of your Terraform modules. Here are key points to consider:

Specificity
> Clearly state what went wrong. Our examples specify strictly what instance types or environments are allowed.

Guidance
> Provide information on how to correct the error. Our messages include examples of valid inputs.

Context
> When relevant, include why the restriction exists. This helps users understand the reasoning behind the validation.

Consistency
    Maintain a consistent style across all error messages in your module.

Clarity
    Use plain language and avoid jargon when possible.

Best practices for error messages:

Be positive
    Frame messages in a constructive way. Instead of `"Invalid input"`, try `"Please provide a valid input"`.

Be concise
    Keep messages short and to the point while still providing necessary information.

Use correct terminology
    Ensure you use the correct technical terms, especially when referencing cloud provider-specific concepts.

Consider internationalization
    If your module might be used globally, consider how your error messages might be translated.

Test your messages
    Have someone unfamiliar with your module try to use it and see if they understand the error messages.

Remember, good error messages can significantly reduce the time users spend troubleshooting and improve the overall user experience of your Terraform modules.

3.14 Consuming Data Across Terraform States

Problem

In complex infrastructure setups, you often need to reference resources or outputs from other Terraform states. This is common in modular architectures or when working with multiple environments. In complex infrastructure setups, it's often necessary to reference resources or outputs from other Terraform states. This is particularly common in modular architectures or when working with multiple environments. Figure 3-4 demonstrates how data is consumed across different Terraform states.

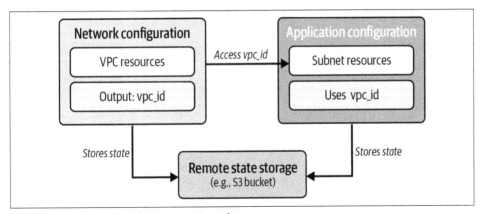

Figure 3-4. Consuming data across Terraform states

Solution

Use Terraform's data sources, particularly the `terraform_remote_state` data source, to access information from other Terraform states. However, first consider using other less sensitive data sources when possible.

Here's an example using AWS data sources and then `terraform_remote_state`:

```
# First, try to use cloud-native data sources
data "aws_vpc" "existing" {
  tags = {
    Environment = "production"
  }
}

output "vpc_id" {
  value = data.aws_vpc.existing.id
}

# If necessary, use terraform_remote_state
data "terraform_remote_state" "network" {
  backend = "s3"

  config = {
    bucket = "my-terraform-state"
    key    = "network/terraform.tfstate"
    region = "us-west-2"
  }
}

resource "aws_subnet" "example" {
  vpc_id     = data.terraform_remote_state.network.outputs.vpc_id
  cidr_block = "10.0.1.0/24"
}
```

Discussion

When consuming data across Terraform states, consider the following points:

Data source priority
> Whenever possible, use cloud native data sources (such as `aws_vpc` in the example) before resorting to `terraform_remote_state`. This approach is often more direct and avoids exposing potentially sensitive information from your state files.

Remote state usage
> The `terraform_remote_state` data source is powerful but should be used judiciously. It allows you to access outputs from another Terraform state, which is useful for modular architectures.

Backend configuration
> Ensure your backend (such as `s3` in the example) is properly configured and secured. Use appropriate access controls and consider enabling versioning and encryption.

Sensitive information
> Be cautious about what information you expose through state outputs, as anyone with access to the state can view this data.

State locking
> Ensure your backend supports state locking to prevent concurrent modifications that could lead to state inconsistencies.

Version compatibility
> Be aware of version differences between your referencing state and your current configuration. Outputs might change between versions.

Error Handling
> Consider using the `try` function when accessing remote state outputs to handle cases where the output might not exist:

```
vpc_id = try(data.terraform_remote_state.network.outputs.vpc_id, null)
```

By carefully considering these points, you can effectively share information across your Terraform configurations while maintaining security and flexibility in your infrastructure management.

## CHAPTER 4

Terraform Modules and Providers

Modules in Terraform are self-contained packages of Terraform configurations that are managed as a group. They are used to encapsulate code into reusable components and to organize code to facilitate teamwork and collaboration. Each module can include several resources that are configured to work together.

Modules can be compared to functions in traditional programming languages. Like a function, a module encapsulates a code block with a specific purpose and can be reused in different contexts. However, unlike a function, a module manages a collection of resources rather than performing computation.

Terraform modules are created using the same language syntax as the root-level Terraform configurations (.tf files). Using the module configuration block, they can be called from within other modules or the root module.

While modules help us organize resources and reuse code, Terraform Providers interact with external APIs to create, read, update, and delete those resources. Each provider is responsible for understanding API interactions and exposing resources.

Terraform is compatible with many cloud providers, including AWS, GCP, Microsoft Azure, and other service providers such as GitHub, Datadog, and many others.

4.1 Using Public Modules to Create an EKS Cluster

Problem

You have set up a VPC within AWS, and now you'd like to start hosting some applications on Kubernetes. You want to set up an Elastic Kubernetes Service (EKS) cluster and get it configured for the first time.

Solution

Using the public AWS EKS module on the Terraform Registry, you can efficiently set up your infrastructure with code configuration, which is what you need to get your Kubernetes cluster running on AWS. First, ensure you have an AWS account and the necessary permissions to create EKS clusters. Then, browse the Terraform Registry to find the module we'll be using by searching for "terraform-aws-modules eks."

The Terraform Registry shows documentation for the module (see Figure 4-1), what inputs are required, what outputs are provided, and other dependencies and resources available to us as we use the module.

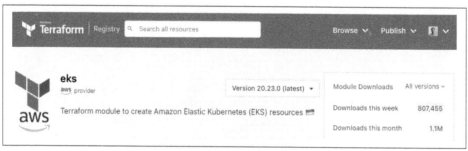

Figure 4-1. Terraform Registry AWS EKS Terraform module listing

Since we're building off the previous recipe we used for the VPC module in Chapter 3, we don't have to respecify the AWS provider or create the VPC module again.

Our *variables.tf* file is mainly set up, but there are more variables we have to add, like the Kubernetes version we want to use and how we want to configure our worker node pool that is going to host our applications as we add them to our EKS cluster.

First, let's add these values to our *variables.tf* file, which will be necessary for all the inputs we need for using the EKS module:

```
variable "cluster_version" {
  type        = string
  description = "The Kubernetes version for our clusters"
  default     = "1.30"
}

variable "cluster_instance_type" {
  type        = string
  description = "EC2 instance type for the EKS autoscaling group."
  default     = "m5.large"
}

variable "cluster_asg_desired_capacity" {
  type        = number
  description = "The default number of EC2 instances our EKS cluster runs."
  default     = 3
}

variable "cluster_asg_max_size" {
```

```
  type         = number
  description = "The maximum number of EC2 instances our EKS cluster will have."
  default     = 5
}

variable "cluster_enabled_log_types" {
  type         = list(string)
  description = "The log types that will be enabled for the EKS cluster."
  default     = ["api", "audit", "authenticator", "controllerManager", "scheduler"]
}

variable "cluster_write_kubeconfig" {
  type         = bool
  description = "Toggle to output a Kubernetes configuration file. "
  default     = false
}
```

Next, let's set up a Key Management Service (KMS) key for encrypting and securing our secrets within Kubernetes. Add a *kms.tf* file to your project with the following configuration:

```
resource "aws_kms_key" "eks" {
  description             = "EKS Secret Encryption Key"
  deletion_window_in_days = 7
  enable_key_rotation     = true
}
```

Now, let's set up the EKS cluster by passing the defined variables and the KMS key details and working with Terraform's data sources to authenticate to our EKS cluster:

```
data "aws_eks_cluster" "cluster" {
  name = module.eks.cluster_id
}

data "aws_eks_cluster_auth" "cluster" {
  name = module.eks.cluster_id
}

provider "kubernetes" {
  host                   = data.aws_eks_cluster.cluster.endpoint
  cluster_ca_certificate = base64decode(data.aws_eks_cluster.cluster.ca.0.data)
  token                  = data.aws_eks_cluster_auth.cluster.token
}

module "eks" {
  source          = "terraform-aws-modules/eks/aws"
  version         = "20.24.0"
  cluster_name    = var.project_name
  cluster_version = var.cluster_version
  subnets         = module.vpc.private_subnets
  vpc_id          = module.vpc.vpc_id

  cluster_enabled_log_types = var.cluster_enabled_log_types
  write_kubeconfig          = var.cluster_write_kubeconfig

  cluster_encryption_config = [
    {
      provider_key_arn = aws_kms_key.eks.arn
      resources        = ["secrets"]
    }
  ]
```

```
  worker_groups = [
    {
      asg_desired_capacity = var.cluster_asg_desired_capacity
      asg_max_size         = var.cluster_asg_max_size
      instance_type        = var.cluster_instance_type
    }
  ]
}
```

Now that we have all our Terraform configurations, we can call `terraform init` to download our dependencies and create our Terraform lockfile.

Discussion

In this example, we've used Terraform's public module registry to create an EKS cluster that we can use and extend. Here's a breakdown of what we've done:

- We've defined variables for our EKS cluster, including the Kubernetes version, instance type, autoscaling group settings, and logging configurations.
- We've set up a KMS key for encrypting secrets within Kubernetes, enhancing the security of our cluster.
- We've used the `terraform-aws-modules/eks/aws` module to create our EKS cluster, passing in our defined variables and configurations.
- We've set up the Kubernetes provider to authenticate with our newly created EKS cluster.

One important note about this cluster is that we shouldn't use Terraform for configuration management or deploying applications to the cluster. It's best to keep the EKS authentication and instantiation separate from the configuration of applications running on the cluster. This separation allows for easier maintenance and upgrades.

If you apply this code, you can use `terraform destroy` to remove the cluster when you're done experimenting or if you need to make significant changes. Remember to always review the created resources and associated costs before applying Terraform configurations in a production environment.

4.2 Linting Terraform with GitHub Actions

Problem

Ensuring that your Terraform configuration is linted correctly and runs as expected can be challenging, especially as you maintain your code over time or work with larger teams. You need an automated way to check your Terraform files for potential errors, best practices adherence, and code style consistency. Figure 4-2 illustrates a typical linting process for Terraform code, showing how automated checks can identify issues before they make it into production.

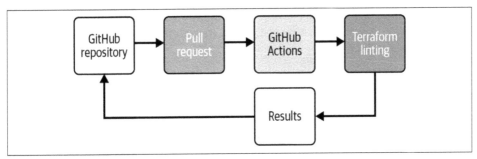

Figure 4-2. Linting Terraform with GitHub Actions

Solution

Using GitHub Actions and a dash of YAML configuration, we can create a workflow that automatically lints your Terraform code, along with other types of files in your repository. We'll use Super-Linter, a robust tool that includes linters for multiple languages and file types, including Terraform.

To start this process, you must have a GitHub account and have GitHub Actions enabled on the repository where you'll be pushing your code. You will need an existing Terraform configuration to test this recipe. Once you have chosen your Terraform configuration repository, create a *.github/workflows* directory at the root of your repository. Then, create a *superlinter.yml* file in the workflows folder with the following content:

```yaml
name: "Code Quality: Super-Linter"

on:
  pull_request:

jobs:
  superlinter:
    name: Super-Linter
    runs-on: ubuntu-latest
    steps:
      - name: Checkout Repository
        uses: actions/checkout@v3
        with:
          fetch-depth: 1

      - name: Lint Code
        uses: github/super-linter:v4
        env:
          VALIDATE_ALL_CODEBASE: true
          DEFAULT_BRANCH: "main"
          DISABLE_ERRORS: false
          VALIDATE_TERRAFORM: true
          VALIDATE_YAML: true
          VALIDATE_JSON: true
          VALIDATE_MD: true
```

This GitHub Action workflow will ensure that your Terraform, YAML, JSON, and Markdown files have been formatted correctly. This code will run during pull requests, helping to catch formatting issues before they enter your main branch. Next, let's add a specific Terraform validation step. Create a *terraform.yml* file in the same workflows directory:

```
name: "Terraform Validation"

on:
  push:
    branches:
      - main
  pull_request:

jobs:
  terraform:
    name: Terraform
    runs-on: ubuntu-latest
    steps:
      - name: Checkout Repository
        uses: actions/checkout@v2

      - name: Setup Terraform
        uses: hashicorp/setup-terraform@v1

      - name: Terraform Format
        run: terraform fmt -check -recursive

      - name: Terraform Init
        run: terraform init

      - name: Terraform Validate
        run: terraform validate
```

This workflow will run Terraform-specific checks, including formatting, initialization, and validation. Please see the visual in Figure 4-3.

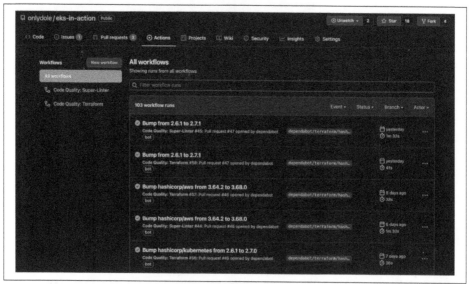

Figure 4-3. GitHub Actions workflows providing Terraform feedback loops

Discussion

These two GitHub Actions workflows add significant value by providing automated oversight on your Terraform configuration. Here's what each does:

- The Super-Linter workflow:
  - Checks multiple file types, including Terraform, for style and syntax issues
  - Runs on pull requests to catch issues early in the development process
  - Can be extended to check additional file types or apply different rules
- The Terraform-specific workflow:
  - Checks Terraform formatting using `terraform fmt`
  - Initializes the Terraform working directory
  - Validates the Terraform files for correctness
  - Runs on both pushes to the main branch and pull requests

By implementing these workflows, you can:

- Catch errors and style issues early in the development process
- Ensure consistency across your Terraform configurations
- Reduce the time spent on manual code reviews for formatting and basic validation issues
- Improve the overall quality and maintainability of your IaC

Remember, while these automated checks are valuable, they don't replace the need for thorough code reviews and testing. They should be part of your Terraform configurations' comprehensive quality assurance process.

 Implementing linting and validation early in your Terraform development process is a good practice. To ensure code quality, consider setting up these GitHub Actions workflows when creating your Terraform repository.

4.3 Authentication for Terraform Providers

Problem

You need to configure Terraform to authenticate with your infrastructure provider securely.

Solution

While this section appears later in the chapter, authentication is a fundamental concept typically set up at the beginning of your Terraform project. Let's look at how to authenticate with the AWS provider using Terraform variables:

```
provider "aws" {
  region     = "us-west-2"
  access_key = var.aws_access_key
  secret_key = var.aws_secret_key
}

variable "aws_access_key" {
  description = "Access key for AWS provider"
  type        = string
  sensitive   = true
}

variable "aws_secret_key" {
  description = "Secret key for AWS provider"
  type        = string
  sensitive   = true
}
```

Discussion

Providers are a fundamental element of Terraform and are responsible for understanding API interactions and exposing resources. Terraform requires authentication to interact with an infrastructure provider.

In this HCL code, we're authenticating with the AWS provider. AWS uses an access key and a secret key for programmatic access. For security purposes, we are using Terraform variables (var.aws_access_key and var.aws_secret_key) for the access_key and secret_key arguments to avoid hardcoding sensitive data into our Terraform configuration.

These variables are marked as sensitive to prevent the values from being shown in logs or console output. The values for these variables should be provided through the CLI when running Terraform or via a *.tfvars* file not committed to version control.

However, while this method is better than hardcoding credentials, it's not the most secure or recommended practice for production environments. Here are some better practices for managing provider authentication:

Environment variables
> Use environment variables to set credentials. For AWS, you can use AWS_ACCESS _KEY_ID and AWS_SECRET_ACCESS_KEY.

Shared credentials file
> AWS CLI uses a shared credentials file at ~/.aws/credentials. Terraform can use this same file.

IAM roles

If running Terraform from an EC2 instance, you can assign an IAM role to the instance, which Terraform can use automatically.

AWS Vault

A tool that securely stores and accesses AWS credentials in a development environment.

HashiCorp Vault

A secrets management tool that can dynamically generate AWS credentials.

Here's an example of using shared credentials:

```
provider "aws" {
  region                  = "us-west-2"
  shared_credentials_file = "~/.aws/credentials"
  profile                 = "dev"
}
```

Remember, each provider has its way of handling authentication. For example, the Azure provider uses either a service principal or Managed Service Identity (MSI). Always refer to the specific provider's documentation for authentication best practices.

Finally, never commit sensitive information like access keys to version control. Always use a combination of variables, environment variables, or secure secret management tools to handle sensitive data in your Terraform configurations.

4.4 Authentication for Private Modules

Problem

You need to configure Terraform to authenticate with a private module registry to consume private modules.

Solution

To use private modules in Terraform, you need to authenticate with the private registry. Here's how you can set this up:

1. Specify the private module in your Terraform configuration:

```
# Specify the required providers
terraform {
  required_providers {
    aws = {
      source  = "hashicorp/aws"
      version = "~> 5.0"
    }
  }
}
```

```
# Use a private module from Terraform Cloud
# Replace 'my-org' with your organization name
# Replace 'my-module' with your module name
module "my_module" {
  source  = "app.terraform.io/my-org/my-module"
  version = "1.0.0"
}

# Example usage of a private VPC module
module "vpc" {
  source  = "app.terraform.io/my-company/vpc/aws"
  version = "1.0.0"

  vpc_cidr = "10.0.0.0/16"
  azs      = ["us-west-2a", "us-west-2b", "us-west-2c"]
}
```

2. To authenticate, you need to provide credentials. This can be done in two ways:

   a. Using a credentials block in the CLI configuration file (*~/.terraformrc* on Linux/MacOS, *%APPDATA%\terraform.rc* on Windows):

   ```
   credentials "app.terraform.io" {
     token = "your-api-token"
   }
   ```

   b. By setting the TERRAFORM_CONFIG environment variable to point to a separate credentials file:

   ```
   export TERRAFORM_CONFIG=/path/to/terraform.rc
   ```

   where /path/to/terraform.rc contains:

   ```
   credentials "app.terraform.io" {
     token = "your-api-token"
   }
   ```

Discussion

Private modules provide reusable, standard infrastructure patterns that are only accessible to you and your organization. They are usually stored in a private module registry such as HCP Terraform's private module registry.

When using private modules, Terraform needs to authenticate with the private registry. This is typically done using an HCP Terraform API token. Here are some key points to remember:

Token security
> The API token is sensitive information. Never commit it to version control or share it insecurely. Use environment variables or secure secret management tools to handle the token.

Token permissions
> Ensure the token has the necessary permissions to access the private modules you're using. In HCP Terraform, you can create tokens with specific permissions.

CI/CD integration

>   If you're using Terraform in a CI/CD pipeline, you'll need to securely provide the token to your build environment. Many CI/CD platforms offer secure ways to manage secrets.

Token rotation

>   Regularly rotate your API tokens as a security best practice. Update your Terraform configurations or environment variables when you do.

Least privilege

>   Use tokens with the minimum necessary permissions. For example, if you're only reading modules, use a token that only has read permissions.

Remember, the authentication method may vary if you use a private registry other than HCP Terraform. Always consult the documentation of your specific registry for the most up-to-date authentication methods.

4.5 Creating a Terraform Module

Problem

You need to create a reusable Terraform module for a specific set of resources to be used in various environments or projects.

Solution

Here's an example of how to create a basic Terraform module for provisioning an AWS EC2 instance:

```
# File: main.tf

# Define the EC2 instance resource
resource "aws_instance" "example" {
  ami           = var.ami
  instance_type = var.instance_type

  tags = {
    Name = var.instance_name
  }
}

# File: variables.tf

# Define input variables for the module
variable "ami" {
  description = "The AMI to use for the EC2 instance"
  type        = string
}

variable "instance_type" {
  description = "The type of EC2 instance to launch"
  type        = string
  default     = "t2.micro"
```

```
}

variable "instance_name" {
  description = "The Name tag for the EC2 instance"
  type        = string
}

# File: outputs.tf

# Define outputs from the module
output "instance_id" {
  description = "The ID of the instance"
  value       = aws_instance.example.id
}

output "instance_public_ip" {
  description = "The public IP address of the instance"
  value       = aws_instance.example.public_ip
}
```

To use this module, you would call it in another Terraform configuration file:

```
module "ec2_instance" {
  source        = "./my_module"
  ami           = "ami-abc123"
  instance_type = "t2.micro"
  instance_name = "my-instance"
}

output "instance_id" {
  value = module.ec2_instance.instance_id
}

output "instance_public_ip" {
  value = module.ec2_instance.instance_public_ip
}
```

Discussion

Modules in Terraform are self-contained packages of Terraform configurations that manage a collection of related resources. They are used to create reusable components, improve organization, and treat pieces of infrastructure as a cohesive unit.

Our example shows a simple module that creates an AWS EC2 instance. The module is composed of three files:

main.tf

This is where the resources that the module will create are defined. In our example, it creates an aws_instance.

variables.tf

This file defines the input variables used in the main.tf. Variables make your module flexible and usable in different contexts.

```
outputs.tf
```
This file defines the values the module will return to the calling code. It helps return IDs, names, or other attributes of the resources that the module creates.

Key points to remember when creating modules:

- Modules should be focused on a specific task or group of related resources.
- Use variables to make your module flexible and reusable across different environments.
- Provide useful outputs that allow users of your module to access important information about the created resources.
- Document your module by including a *README.md* file that explains what the module does, its inputs, outputs, and any other relevant information.
- Consider versioning your modules, especially if they're shared across teams or projects.

For testing modules, you can create a test directory in your module with example configurations that use the module. This allows you to verify that the module works as expected and provides examples for users of your module:

```
my_module/
├── main.tf
├── variables.tf
├── outputs.tf
├── README.md
└── tests/
    └── example_usage.tf
```

By creating well-structured, reusable modules, you can significantly improve the maintainability and consistency of your Terraform configurations across different projects and environments.

4.6 Managing GitHub Secrets with Terraform

Problem

You want to manage GitHub secrets for your repository using Terraform.

Solution

Here's how to set up the GitHub provider and manage secrets using Terraform:

```
# Configure the GitHub provider
provider "github" {
  token = var.github_token  # Your GitHub personal access token
  owner = var.github_owner  # Your GitHub username or organization name
}

# Define a GitHub secret
```

```
resource "github_actions_secret" "example_secret" {
  repository      = var.github_repository
  secret_name     = "MY_SECRET"
  plaintext_value = var.my_secret
}

# Input variables
variable "github_token" {
  description = "GitHub personal access token"
  type        = string
  sensitive   = true
}

variable "github_owner" {
  description = "GitHub owner (username or organization)"
  type        = string
}

variable "github_repository" {
  description = "GitHub repository name"
  type        = string
}

variable "my_secret" {
  description = "The value of the GitHub secret"
  type        = string
  sensitive   = true
}
```

Discussion

This Terraform configuration allows you to manage GitHub secrets programmatically. Here's a breakdown of what's happening:

GitHub provider
> The GitHub provider is configured with your personal access token and the owner (your username or organization name). This allows Terraform to interact with the GitHub API.

Secret resource
> The github_actions_secret resource defines a secret in your GitHub repository. You specify the repository name, the secret name, and its value.

Variables
> We use variables for sensitive information (like the GitHub token and secret value) and for values that might change between different uses of this configuration (like the repository name).

Key points to remember:

Security
> The github_token and my_secret variables are marked as sensitive. This prevents their values from being displayed in console output or logs.

Token permissions

Ensure your GitHub token has the necessary permissions to manage secrets in the repository.

Secret management

While this method allows you to manage secrets with Terraform, be cautious about storing secret values in your Terraform state. Consider using a secure secret management system in conjunction with this approach.

Idempotency

Terraform will manage the life cycle of these secrets. If you run `terraform apply` multiple times, it will only update the secrets if there are changes.

Version control

While you should commit your Terraform configuration files, never commit files containing actual secret values (such as *.tfvars* files with sensitive data) to version control.

This approach provides a way to version control the existence and names of your secrets while still keeping the actual secret values secure. It's particularly useful in CI/CD pipelines where you need to ensure certain secrets exist in your GitHub repositories.

Remember to handle the Terraform state file securely, as it will contain the plain-text values of your secrets. Consider using remote state with encryption enabled when managing sensitive data like this.

4.7 Managing GitHub Repositories with Terraform

Problem

You need to create and manage GitHub repositories using Terraform.

Solution

In Recipe 4.6, we set up the GitHub authentication. Now let's dig into how we can work specifically with GitHub repositories and set up default options for the code we plan to work with:

```
# Configure the GitHub provider
provider "github" {
  token = var.github_token
  owner = var.github_owner
}

# Create a GitHub repository
resource "github_repository" "example" {
  name        = "example-repo"
  description = "Repository created and managed by Terraform"
```

```
    visibility  = "private"
    auto_init   = true

    template {
      owner      = "github"
      repository = "terraform-module-template"
    }

    topics = ["terraform", "infrastructure-as-code"]

    has_issues    = true
    has_wiki      = true
    has_downloads = false

    allow_merge_commit = true
    allow_squash_merge = true
    allow_rebase_merge = false
}

# Input variables
variable "github_token" {
  description = "GitHub personal access token"
  type        = string
  sensitive   = true
}

variable "github_owner" {
  description = "GitHub owner (username or organization)"
  type        = string
}

# Output the repository URL
output "repository_url" {
  value       = github_repository.example.html_url
  description = "URL of the created repository"
}
```

Discussion

This Terraform configuration allows you to create and manage GitHub repositories programmatically. Here's a breakdown of the key components:

GitHub provider

> The GitHub provider is configured with your personal access token and the owner (your username or organization name). This allows Terraform to interact with the GitHub API.

Repository resource

> The github_repository resource defines the characteristics of the GitHub repository you want to create or manage.

Variables

> We use variables for sensitive information (like the GitHub token) and for values that might change between different uses of this configuration (like the owner name).

Output

We define an output to easily retrieve the URL of the created repository.

Key points to remember:

Repository settings

The configuration includes various settings for the repository, such as visibility, initialization, issue tracking, wiki, and merge strategies. Adjust these as needed for your specific requirements.

Template

The template block allows you to create the repository based on a template. This can be useful for standardizing repository structures across your organization.

Topics

You can assign topics to your repository, which can help with categorization and discoverability.

Security

The `github_token` variable is marked as sensitive to prevent its value from being displayed in console output or logs.

Token permissions

Ensure your GitHub token has the necessary permissions to create and manage repositories.

Idempotency

Terraform will manage the life cycle of this repository. If you run `terraform apply` multiple times, it will only update the repository if there are changes in your configuration.

Existing Repositories

If the repository already exists, Terraform will import it into its state and manage it going forward. Be careful not to overwrite existing settings unintentionally.

This approach provides a way to version control your GitHub repository configurations, ensuring consistency across your organization and enabling easy replication of repository structures. It's particularly useful for organizations that need to create and manage many repositories with standardized settings.

Remember to handle the Terraform state file securely, especially if managing private repositories or sensitive configurations. Consider using a remote state with encryption enabled when managing GitHub resources.

4.8 Dynamic Configuration with Consul KV

Problem

You must store and retrieve key-value pairs from HashiCorp Consul's key-value (KV) store to use as dynamic configuration in your Terraform code. This is particularly useful when you need to pass dependencies across different Terraform states or when you want to externalize configuration that might change frequently. Figure 4-4 demonstrates the flow of information in a Consul key-value configuration setup. This diagram illustrates how Terraform interacts with Consul to store and retrieve dynamic configuration data, enabling more flexible and centralized management of infrastructure parameters.

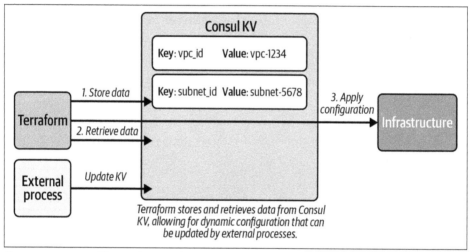

Figure 4-4. Consul key-value configuration flows

Solution

Here's an example of how to use Consul KV with Terraform to store and retrieve a VPC ID:

```
# Configure the Consul provider
provider "consul" {
  address = "localhost:8500"
  scheme  = "http"
}

# Store the VPC ID in Consul KV
resource "consul_key_prefix" "vpc" {
  path_prefix = "terraform/vpc/"

  subkeys = {
    "id" = aws_vpc.main.id
  }
}
```

```
# Retrieve the VPC ID from Consul KV
data "consul_keys" "vpc" {
  key {
    name = "vpc_id"
    path = "terraform/vpc/id"
  }
}

# Use the retrieved VPC ID
resource "aws_subnet" "example" {
  vpc_id     = data.consul_keys.vpc.var.vpc_id
  cidr_block = "10.0.1.0/24"
}
```

Discussion

This Terraform configuration demonstrates how to use Consul's KV store for dynamic configuration. Here's a breakdown of what's happening:

Consul provider
> We configure the Consul provider with the address of our Consul server. Adjust this as needed for your Consul setup.

Storing data
> The `consul_key_prefix` resource is used to store the VPC ID in Consul's KV store. In this example, we're storing the ID of a VPC that we've created (represented by `aws_vpc.main.id`).

Retrieving data
> The `consul_keys` data source is used to retrieve the VPC ID from Consul. This allows us to use the stored value in other parts of our Terraform configuration.

Using retrieved data
> We use the retrieved VPC ID when creating a subnet, demonstrating how this data can be used in resource creation.

Key points to remember:

Consul setup
> This solution assumes you have Consul set up and running. Setting up Consul is beyond the scope of this recipe, but it's a prerequisite for using this configuration.

Key namespacing
> We use a path prefix (`terraform/vpc/`) to namespace our keys. This is a good practice to organize your keys, especially if you're using Consul for multiple purposes.

Data persistence
> Consul KV allows you to persist data outside of Terraform's state. This can be useful for sharing data between different Terraform configurations or runs.

Dynamic configuration
> This approach allows you to change values in Consul and have those changes reflected in your Terraform runs without modifying the Terraform code itself.

Security
> Ensure that your Consul setup is properly secured, especially if you're storing sensitive information. Consider using ACLs and encryption.

Consul versus Terraform state
> While this approach can be useful, it's important to understand the trade-offs. Terraform state is designed to track resource dependencies, while Consul KV is more suited for dynamic, shared configuration.

This pattern is particularly useful in scenarios where:

- You need to share data between different Terraform configurations or modules.
- You want to externalize configuration that might change frequently.
- You're building a system where other processes might update configuration that Terraform needs to consume.

Remember, while this provides flexibility, it also introduces an external dependency to your Terraform runs. Ensure that your Consul cluster is reliable and that you have proper error handling in place in case Consul is unavailable.

4.9 Service-Health-Aware Provider Configuration

Problem

You want to configure Terraform providers based on the health status of your service endpoints, ensuring that your infrastructure deployment uses healthy services. Figure 4-5 provides a visual representation of how service health awareness is integrated into the provider configuration process. This diagram shows the flow of health check information and how it influences the selection of active service endpoints, ensuring that your infrastructure deployment uses only healthy services.

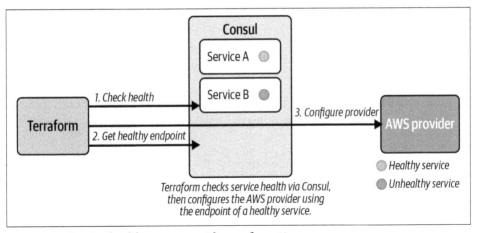

Figure 4-5. Service-health-aware provider configuration

Solution

Here's a Terraform configuration that uses Consul's HTTP API to check service health and configures an AWS provider based on the health check status:

```
# Data source to check service health via Consul HTTP API
data "http" "service_health_check" {
  url = "http://localhost:8500/v1/health/service/my-service"
}

# Local values to process the health check response
locals {
  service_health = jsondecode(data.http.service_health_check.body)[0]
  active_node    = local.service_health.Status == "passing" ? local.service_health.Service.Address :
    "fallback_address"
}

# Configure the AWS provider using the health check result
provider "aws" {
  region   = "us-west-2"
  endpoint = local.active_node
}

# Example resource using the configured provider
resource "aws_instance" "example" {
  ami           = "ami-0c55b159cbfafe1f0"
  instance_type = "t2.micro"
}
```

Discussion

This configuration demonstrates how to make Terraform provider configuration dynamic based on service health. Here's a breakdown of the key components:

Health check data source
> The http data source is used to query Consul's HTTP API for the health status of a specific service (my-service in this example).

Response processing
> The jsondecode function is used to parse the JSON response from Consul. We assume the first service instance is the one we're interested in.

Dynamic endpoint selection
> A ternary operator is used to select either the address of the healthy service or a fallback address, based on the health check status.

Provider configuration
> The AWS provider is configured with the dynamically selected endpoint.

Key points to consider:

Consul dependency
> This solution assumes you have Consul running and that your services are registered with Consul. Adjust the URL in the HTTP data source to match your Consul setup.

Error handling
> This example doesn't include robust error handling. In a production scenario, you'd want to add checks for empty responses, multiple service instances, and potential API failures.

Security
> The example uses an unsecured HTTP call to Consul. In a production environment, you should use HTTPS and proper authentication.

Fallback strategy
> The example uses a simple fallback to a predefined address. In practice, you might want a more sophisticated fallback strategy, possibly querying multiple services or using a default provider configuration.

Provider-specific considerations
> The exact configuration will depend on the provider you're using. Not all providers support dynamic endpoint configuration in the same way.

Timing and caching
> Remember that this health check happens during Terraform's planning and apply phases. It doesn't continuously monitor service health during execution.

This pattern is particularly useful in scenarios where:

- You have multiple service endpoints and want to use the healthy ones automatically.
- You're implementing a form of failover or high availability in your infrastructure provisioning.
- You want to ensure that Terraform operations only proceed when dependent services are healthy.

While this approach provides flexibility, it also introduces complexity and external dependencies into your Terraform workflow. Ensure that your health checking mechanism is reliable and that you have appropriate error handling and logging.

4.10 Consuming Terraform State with Providers

Problem

You need to access and use the Terraform state from one configuration in another configuration, allowing you to share information between separate Terraform projects or modules.

Solution

First, you must ensure that the state from the first configuration is stored in a backend that the second configuration can access:

```
# Configure the backend where the state is stored
terraform {
  backend "s3" {
    bucket = "my-terraform-state-bucket"
    key    = "network/terraform.tfstate"
    region = "us-west-2"
  }
}

# Data source to access the remote state
data "terraform_remote_state" "network" {
  backend = "s3"
  config = {
    bucket = "my-terraform-state-bucket"
    key    = "network/terraform.tfstate"
    region = "us-west-2"
  }
}

# Example resource using data from the remote state
resource "aws_instance" "app_server" {
  ami           = "ami-0c55b159cbfafe1f0"
  instance_type = "t2.micro"
  subnet_id     = data.terraform_remote_state.network.outputs.subnet_id

  tags = {
```

```
      Name = "AppServerInstance"
  }
}

# Output demonstrating access to the remote state
output "vpc_id" {
  value = data.terraform_remote_state.network.outputs.vpc_id
}
```

Discussion

This configuration shows how to consume Terraform state from one configuration in another. Here's a breakdown of the key components:

Backend configuration
> The `terraform` block configures the backend where the state is stored. In this example, we're using an S3 backend.

Remote state data source
> The `terraform_remote_state` data source is used to access the outputs from another Terraform configuration's state.

Resource creation
> We create an AWS EC2 instance, using the `subnet_id` output from the remote state.

Output
> We demonstrate how to access and output a value (`vpc_id`) from the remote state.

Key points to consider:

State storage
> Ensure that your state is stored in a backend that's accessible to both configurations. S3 is a common choice, but Terraform supports various backend types.

State isolation
> While sharing state can be useful, it's important to maintain proper separation of concerns. Only share what's necessary between configurations.

Version control
> The remote state feature allows you to version control your infrastructure more effectively by breaking it into smaller, manageable pieces.

Security
> Be mindful of the permissions required to access the remote state. Ensure that your backend is properly secured and that access is restricted as necessary.

Dependency management

Using remote state creates implicit dependencies between your Terraform configurations. Be aware of these dependencies and manage them carefully.

Read-only access

The `terraform_remote_state` data source provides read-only access to the state. You can't modify the remote state through this method.

Performance

Accessing remote state adds some overhead to your Terraform operations. This is usually negligible but could be noticeable for very large states or slow network connections.

This pattern is particularly useful in scenarios where:

- You want to separate your infrastructure into logical components (e.g., networking, compute, database) while still allowing them to reference each other.
- You need to share information between different teams or projects without tightly coupling their Terraform configurations.
- You're implementing a layered or modular approach to your infrastructure as code.

Remember that while consuming remote state can be powerful, it also introduces coupling between your Terraform configurations. Use this feature judiciously and always consider the trade-offs between sharing state and maintaining isolation between different parts of your infrastructure.

4.11 Using Multiple, Identical Providers

Problem

You need to manage resources across multiple regions or accounts using the same provider type in a single Terraform configuration.

Solution

Here's a Terraform configuration that demonstrates how to use multiple AWS providers to manage resources in different regions:

```
# Configure the default AWS provider
provider "aws" {
  region = "us-west-2"
}

# Configure an additional AWS provider for the US East region
provider "aws" {
  alias  = "east"
```

```
    region = "us-east-1"
}

# EC2 instance in the default region (us-west-2)
resource "aws_instance" "west_server" {
  ami           = "ami-0c55b159cbfafe1f0"
  instance_type = "t2.micro"

  tags = {
    Name = "WestServerInstance"
  }
}

# EC2 instance in the US East region
resource "aws_instance" "east_server" {
  provider      = aws.east
  ami           = "ami-0747bdcabd34c712a"
  instance_type = "t2.micro"

  tags = {
    Name = "EastServerInstance"
  }
}

# S3 bucket in the default region
resource "aws_s3_bucket" "west_bucket" {
  bucket = "my-west-bucket-12345"
}

# S3 bucket in the US East region
resource "aws_s3_bucket" "east_bucket" {
  provider = aws.east
  bucket   = "my-east-bucket-67890"
}
```

Discussion

This configuration demonstrates how to use multiple instances of the same provider (in this case, AWS) to manage resources across different regions. Here's a breakdown of the key components:

Default provider
> The first AWS provider block configures the default provider, which will be used when no specific provider is referenced.

Additional provider
> The second AWS provider block sets up an additional provider with an alias ("east") for the US East region.

Resource creation
> We create EC2 instances and S3 buckets in both regions, demonstrating how to specify which provider to use for each resource.

Key points to consider:

Provider aliases
> The `alias` argument in the provider block allows you to create multiple instances of the same provider with different configurations.

Resource provider specification
> For resources using a nondefault provider, you need to specify the provider using the provider argument, referencing it as `aws.east` (where `"east"` is the alias).

Region-specific AMIs
> We use different AMI IDs for the EC2 instances in different regions. AMIs are region-specific, so you must ensure you use the correct AMI for each region.

Naming conventions
> It's a good practice to use clear naming conventions for resources created in different regions or accounts to avoid confusion.

State management
> While this configuration manages resources across regions, all of these resources are still in the same Terraform state. Consider whether this is appropriate for your use case or if you need separate states.

IAM and permissions
> Ensure that the credentials used have the necessary permissions in all regions where you create resources.

Increased complexity
> While this approach is powerful, it can increase the complexity of your Terraform configuration. Use it judiciously.

This pattern is particularly useful in scenarios where:

- You must deploy similar infrastructure across multiple regions for redundancy or global distribution.
- You're managing resources across different AWS accounts.
- You want to compare or test configurations across different regions.

Remember that while this approach allows you to manage multiregion or multiaccount resources in a single configuration, it's not always the best solution. Consider using separate Terraform configurations for each region or Terraform workspaces for complex multiregion setups.

## CHAPTER 5

Container Management with Terraform

This chapter explores the application of Terraform in managing containers, which are instrumental in the modern paradigm of developing, packaging, and deploying applications to ensure consistency across diverse environments. Terraform engages with renowned container orchestration platforms such as Kubernetes and Docker via its provider plug-ins. These plug-ins extend Terraform's capabilities, enabling the management of resources within these orchestration platforms.

The interaction between Terraform and these platforms allows for the automation of provisioning and managing containerized applications and the infrastructure they operate on. For instance, with the Kubernetes provider, Terraform can manage resources such as Pods, services, and others, while the Docker provider enables the management of Docker images and containers.

Utilizing Terraform for container management streamlines the infrastructure development process, bringing about benefits akin to application code management, such as version control, peer review, and automated testing. Whether orchestrating Docker containers or administrating a Kubernetes cluster, Terraform offers a coherent and scalable approach to managing containerized applications, aligning infrastructure management with modern development practices.

5.1 Using Local Versus Remote Docker Images

Problem

You have Docker images both locally and in a remote Docker registry, and you need to decide when to use each one. You want to deploy containers from these images using Terraform.

Solution

We can distinguish between local and remote Docker containers that we run, so let's dive into how we can do that:

```
# Configure the Docker provider
provider "docker" {}

# Use a remote Docker image
resource "docker_image" "remote_image" {
  name = "<REMOTE_IMAGE_NAME>:<TAG>"
}

resource "docker_container" "remote_container" {
  name  = "remote_container"
  image = docker_image.remote_image.latest
}

# Use a local Docker image
resource "docker_image" "local_image" {
  name        = "<LOCAL_IMAGE_NAME>:<TAG>"
  keep_locally = true
}

resource "docker_container" "local_container" {
  name  = "local_container"
  image = docker_image.local_image.latest
}
```

Discussion

In this solution, we're deploying Docker containers from local and remote images using the Docker provider:

- The provider "docker" block initializes the Docker provider.
- The resource "docker_image" "remote_image" block pulls a Docker image from a remote Docker registry.
- The resource "docker_container" "remote_container" block deploys a Docker container from the pulled remote Docker image.
- The resource "docker_image" "local_image" block loads a locally present Docker image. The keep_locally attribute is set to true to prevent Terraform from checking the Docker registry for the image.
- The resource "docker_container" "local_container" block deploys a Docker container from the loaded local Docker image.

In general, you would use a remote Docker image when you want the latest version of an image or when the image isn't available locally. You would use a local Docker image when you want to use a specific version of an image you have locally or when you want to use a custom image you've created and haven't pushed to a Docker registry.

In some enterprise environments, systems may be deliberately configured without public internet access for security reasons. In such cases, local Docker registries might be used to serve containerized applications. However, these disconnected systems may also be unreachable by the host running Terraform, making them unsuitable for management through this method. When working with air-gapped or highly restricted environments, consider alternative deployment and management strategies that align with your organization's security policies.

5.2 Distinguishing Between Cluster Deployment and Cluster Configuration

Problem

You are managing a Kubernetes cluster and need to distinguish between two different operations: cluster deployment and cluster configuration. Deployment refers to creating or launching a cluster, while configuration refers to managing the settings and resources of an already deployed cluster (see Figure 5-1). You need to perform both operations using Terraform.

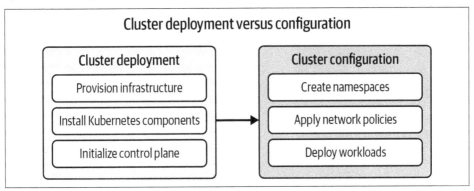

Figure 5-1. Kubernetes cluster creation and configuration differences

Solution

Let's create an EKS in AWS to start deploying workloads and working with containers in this context:

```
# Deploy an EKS cluster
provider "aws" {
  region = "<REGION>"
}

module "eks" {
  source          = "terraform-aws-modules/eks/aws"
  cluster_name    = "my-cluster"
  cluster_version = "1.20"
  subnets         = ["<SUBNET_ID_1>", "<SUBNET_ID_2>", "<SUBNET_ID_3>"]
```

```
  vpc_id           = "<VPC_ID>"

  node_groups = {
    eks_nodes = {
      desired_capacity = 3
      max_capacity     = 10
      min_capacity     = 1
      instance_type    = "t3.medium"
    }
  }
}

# Configure the cluster
provider "kubernetes" {
  host                   = module.eks.cluster_endpoint
  cluster_ca_certificate = base64decode(module.eks.cluster_ca_data)
  token                  = data.aws_eks_cluster_auth.cluster.token
}

data "aws_eks_cluster_auth" "cluster" {
  name = module.eks.cluster_id
}

resource "kubernetes_namespace" "namespace" {
  metadata {
    name = "my-namespace"
  }
}
```

Discussion

In the first part of the solution, we're deploying a Kubernetes cluster on AWS using EKS with the help of the `terraform-aws-modules/eks/aws` module. This is a simple example of a cluster with a desired node group capacity of 3:

- The `provider "aws"` block authenticates with AWS using your default credentials and sets the AWS region.

- The `module "eks"` block sets up the EKS cluster. You must provide the IDs for your VPC and at least one subnet. The `node_groups` parameter sets the configuration for the EKS nodes, including the desired, minimum, and maximum capacity and the instance type.

In the second part, we're configuring the deployed cluster by creating a new namespace using the `kubernetes_namespace` resource:

- The `provider "kubernetes"` block establishes authentication with the deployed EKS cluster. It retrieves the necessary authentication details (cluster endpoint, cluster certificate authority data, and token) from the deployed EKS cluster.

- `data "aws_eks_cluster_auth" "cluster"` retrieves the token for EKS cluster authentication.

- The resource "kubernetes_namespace" "namespace" block creates a new namespace in the Kubernetes cluster.

This solution illustrates the basic difference between deployment and configuration: deployment involves creating the necessary infrastructure (such as the EKS cluster), and configuration involves setting up or modifying settings within the deployed infrastructure (such as creating a new namespace within the cluster).

5.3 Authorizing Terraform for Cluster Operations

Problem

You need to authorize Terraform to perform operations on your Kubernetes cluster. This involves setting up permissions and authentication mechanisms to allow Terraform to interact with your cluster's API.

Solution

Terraform needs to have authorization and authentication to work with containers, especially when using something like Kubernetes. In this example, let's do this with an AWS EKS cluster:

```
provider "aws" {
  region = "<REGION>"
}

data "aws_eks_cluster" "cluster" {
  name = "<CLUSTER_NAME>"
}

data "aws_eks_cluster_auth" "cluster" {
  name = "<CLUSTER_NAME>"
}

provider "kubernetes" {
  host                   = data.aws_eks_cluster.cluster.endpoint
  cluster_ca_certificate = base64decode(data.aws_eks_cluster.cluster.ca.0.data)
  token                  = data.aws_eks_cluster_auth.cluster.token
  load_config_file       = false
}
```

Discussion

In this solution, we're using AWS as the cloud provider and EKS for the Kubernetes cluster:

- The provider "aws" block is used to authenticate with AWS and set the region.
- The data "aws_eks_cluster" "cluster" and data "aws_eks_cluster_auth" "cluster" blocks are used to fetch information about the EKS cluster, including

the endpoint for the Kubernetes API server, the cluster certificate authority data, and the authentication token.

- The `provider "kubernetes"` block is used to authenticate with the Kubernetes cluster:

  — The `host` argument is set to the API server endpoint of the EKS cluster.

  — The `cluster_ca_certificate` argument is set to the certificate authority data for the EKS cluster, which is base64 decoded.

  — The `token` argument is set to the authentication token for the EKS cluster.

  — The `load_config_file` argument is `false` to prevent the provider from loading a local kubeconfig file.

This setup authorizes Terraform to perform operations on the EKS Kubernetes cluster. It's important to note that you must have the necessary IAM permissions in AWS to access the EKS cluster.

5.4 Scheduling Containers on Kubernetes with YAML

Problem

You need to schedule and run Docker containers on a Kubernetes cluster using Terraform. The configuration for the containers should be defined in YAML format.

Solution

This sample shows how to utilize existing YAML manifests that many infrastructure teams already have available, even when not using Terraform to manage IaC:

```
provider "kubernetes" {
  // Configure your Kubernetes provider
}

resource "kubernetes_manifest" "example" {
  provider = kubernetes

  manifest = yamldecode(file("${path.module}/deployment.yaml"))
}
```

And here's an example *deployment.yaml*:

```
apiVersion: apps/v1
kind: Deployment
metadata:
  name: my-app
  labels:
    app: my-app
spec:
  replicas: 3
  selector:
    matchLabels:
```

```
    app: my-app
  template:
    metadata:
      labels:
        app: my-app
    spec:
      containers:
      - name: my-app
        image: my-image:latest
        ports:
        - containerPort: 8080
```

Discussion

This solution uses the `kubernetes_manifest` resource to apply a Kubernetes Deployment defined in a YAML file:

- The `provider "kubernetes"` block is used to authenticate with the Kubernetes cluster. You need to provide the necessary information to connect to your cluster.
- The `resource "kubernetes_manifest" "example"` block applies a Kubernetes Deployment. It uses the `yamldecode` function to read a YAML file and convert it to a map that can be used as the manifest argument.

The *deployment.yaml* file defines a Deployment that runs three replicas of a Docker container. The container runs an image called `my-image:latest` and exposes port 8080.

The `kubernetes_manifest` resource and the `yamldecode` function are available starting from Terraform 0.15 and require the Kubernetes provider version 2.0.0 or later. If you use an older version of Terraform or the Kubernetes provider, you must define your Kubernetes resources directly in HCL instead of using YAML.

In Kubernetes, the term *scheduling* refers to the process of assigning Pods to nodes in the cluster. This is different from the common understanding of scheduling as setting up tasks to run at specific times. When we talk about *deploying* containers in Kubernetes, we're instructing the Kubernetes scheduler to place our containers (in Pods) on appropriate nodes in the cluster.

5.5 Scheduling Containers on Kubernetes with HCL

Problem

You need to deploy and run Docker containers on a Kubernetes cluster using Terraform. The configuration for the containers should be defined directly in HashiCorp configuration language (HCL) format.

Solution

Besides YAML, you can use HCL instead to work with manifests and other configurations in a Kubernetes cluster:

```
provider "kubernetes" {
  // Configure your Kubernetes provider
}

resource "kubernetes_deployment" "example" {
  metadata {
    name = "my-app"
    labels = {
      app = "my-app"
    }
  }

  spec {
    replicas = 3

    selector {
      match_labels = {
        app = "my-app"
      }
    }

    template {
      metadata {
        labels = {
          app = "my-app"
        }
      }

      spec {
        container {
          name  = "my-app"
          image = "my-image:latest"

          port {
            container_port = 8080
          }
        }
      }
    }
  }
}
```

Discussion

In this solution, we're using the `kubernetes_deployment` resource to deploy and run Docker containers on a Kubernetes cluster:

- The `provider "kubernetes"` block is used to authenticate with the Kubernetes cluster. You need to provide the necessary information to connect to your cluster.

- The `resource "kubernetes_deployment" "example"` block creates a Kubernetes Deployment:

- The `metadata` block defines the `name` and `labels` for the Deployment.
- The `spec` block defines the specifications for the Deployment:
  - `replicas` set the number of replicas for the Deployment.
  - The `selector` block specifies how to identify Pods to manage with this Deployment.
  - The `template` block defines the template for the Pods that the Deployment manages. This includes the Pods' metadata and the containers' specifications within the Pods.

This Deployment creates three replicas of a Pod running a Docker container. The container runs an image called `my-image:latest` and exposes port 8080.

Using HCL to define Kubernetes resources directly in Terraform configuration files offers several advantages:

- It allows for better integration with other Terraform resources and data sources.
- You can use Terraform variables, functions, and expressions directly in your Kubernetes resource definitions.
- It provides a consistent language across your infrastructure-as-code setup if you're already using Terraform for other resources.

However, if you have existing YAML manifests or prefer YAML syntax, you can still use the method described in Recipe 5.4 with the `kubernetes_manifest` resource and `yamldecode` function.

5.6 Transmuting Kubernetes YAML into HCL using k2tf

Problem

You have Kubernetes resource definitions in YAML format, and you want to convert them into HashiCorp configuration language (HCL) format to manage these resources using Terraform.

Solution

To convert Kubernetes YAML into HCL, you can use the Terraform console. This method is consistent with how we've introduced the Terraform console in earlier chapters and doesn't rely on external tools:

1. Save your Kubernetes YAML file (e.g., *deployment.yaml*).
2. Open the Terraform console:

```
terraform console
```

3. In the console, use the `file` and `yamldecode` functions to read and parse the YAML, then wrap it in a `kubernetes_manifest` resource:

```
jsonencode(
  {
    resource = {
      kubernetes_manifest = {
        example = {
          manifest = yamldecode(file("deployment.yaml"))
        }
      }
    }
  }
)
```

4. Copy the output and paste it into your Terraform configuration file.

Discussion

This solution uses built-in Terraform functionality to convert Kubernetes YAML into a format that can be used with the `kubernetes_manifest` resource:

- The `file` function reads the contents of the YAML file.
- The `yamldecode` function parses the YAML content into a Terraform object.
- We wrap this in a `kubernetes_manifest` resource structure.
- The `jsonencode` function is used to format the output in a way that's easy to copy and paste into a Terraform configuration file.

After copying the output into your Terraform configuration, you may need to make some minor adjustments:

- Remove the outer braces {}.
- Format the code for readability (you can use `terraform fmt` for this).

This method has several advantages:

- It doesn't require external tools, making it more portable and easier to use in various environments.
- It uses the `kubernetes_manifest` resource, the current recommended way to manage Kubernetes resources in Terraform.
- It maintains consistency with how we've used the Terraform console in earlier parts of the book.

Remember that while this method can convert most Kubernetes resources, some complex scenarios may require manual adjustments. Always review and test the generated Terraform configuration to ensure it behaves as expected.

5.7 Adjusting Annotations for Kubernetes Deployments

Problem

You need to add or update annotations for a Kubernetes Deployment using Terraform. Annotations allow you to attach arbitrary metadata to Kubernetes objects.

Solution

In this example, an annotation with the key `example.com/my-annotation` and the value `my-value` is added to the Deployment:

```
provider "kubernetes" {
  // Configure your Kubernetes provider
}

resource "kubernetes_deployment" "example" {
  metadata {
    name = "my-app"
    annotations = {
      "example.com/my-annotation" = "my-value"
    }
  }

  spec {
    // Deployment spec
  }
}
```

Discussion

This solution uses the `kubernetes_deployment` resource to create a Kubernetes Deployment with a specified annotation:

- The `provider "kubernetes"` block is used to authenticate with the Kubernetes cluster. You need to provide the necessary information to connect to your cluster.
- The `resource "kubernetes_deployment" "example"` block creates a Kubernetes Deployment:
  - The `metadata` block defines the `name` and `annotations` for the Deployment.
  - The `annotations` argument is a map of strings, where each key-value pair represents an annotation.

- The `annotations` argument allows you to attach arbitrary metadata to the Deployment. Annotations can store information relevant to tools and libraries interacting with the Deployment. Some common uses for annotations include:

  — Build information (e.g., Git commit hash, release version)

  — Logging and monitoring configurations

  — Deployment tracking (e.g., rollout status, last updated timestamp)

  — Tool-specific configurations (e.g., Ingress controller settings)

To update an annotation, you can simply change the value for the corresponding key in the `annotations` argument, and Terraform will apply the change to the Deployment.

To remove an annotation, you can remove the corresponding key-value pair from the `annotations` argument, and Terraform will remove the annotation from the Deployment.

It's important to note that annotations are different from labels. While labels are used for selecting and grouping objects, annotations are not used for identification and cannot be used to select objects. They are primarily for nonidentifying metadata and are often used by automated tools and libraries.

5.8 Adjusting Configuration for Kubernetes Deployments

Problem

You need to adjust the configuration for a Kubernetes Deployment using Terraform. You should change things like the image used by the containers, the number of replicas, or the environment variables.

Solution

In this example, the number of replicas is set to 5, the image used by the container is updated to `my-image:v2`, and an environment variable `ENV_VAR_NAME` is set to `new-value`:

```
variable "replica_count" {
  description = "Number of replicas for the deployment"
  type        = number
  default     = 5
}

variable "image_version" {
  description = "Version of the image to use"
  type        = string
  default     = "v2"
}
```

```
provider "kubernetes" {
  // Configure your Kubernetes provider
}

resource "kubernetes_deployment" "example" {
  metadata {
    name = "my-app"
  }

  spec {
    replicas = var.replica_count

    selector {
      match_labels = {
        app = "my-app"
      }
    }

    template {
      metadata {
        labels = {
          app = "my-app"
        }
      }

      spec {
        container {
          name  = "my-app"
          image = "my-image:${var.image_version}"

          env {
            name  = "ENV_VAR_NAME"
            value = "new-value"
          }

          port {
            container_port = 8080
          }
        }
      }
    }
  }
}
```

Discussion

In this solution, we're using the kubernetes_deployment resource to create or update a Kubernetes Deployment:

- We've introduced two variables: replica_count and image_version. These allow for easier configuration changes without modifying the main resource block.
- The provider "kubernetes" block is used to authenticate with the Kubernetes cluster. You need to provide the necessary information to connect to your cluster.
- The resource "kubernetes_deployment" "example" block defines a Kubernetes Deployment:

  — The metadata block defines the name of the Deployment.

— The `spec` block defines the specifications for the Deployment:

  — `replicas` is set using the `var.replica_count` variable.

  — The `selector` block specifies how to identify Pods to manage with this Deployment.

  — The `template` block defines the template for the Pods that the Deployment manages. This includes the metadata for the Pods and the specifications for the containers within the Pods, including the container image (using the `var.image_version` variable), environment variables, and exposed ports.

To adjust the configuration for the Deployment, you can change the values of the variables when applying the Terraform configuration. For example:

```
terraform apply -var="replica_count=3" -var="image_version=v3"
```

This approach offers several benefits:

- It makes the configuration more flexible and reusable.
- It allows for easier testing of different configurations.
- It separates the configuration values from the resource definition, making the code cleaner and more maintainable.
- It facilitates using different values for different environments (dev, staging, production) without changing the main configuration.

Always test your changes in a nonproduction environment before applying them to your production cluster.

5.9 Applying Kubernetes NetworkPolicies with Terraform

Problem

You need to apply a Kubernetes NetworkPolicy using Terraform. NetworkPolicies define how groups of Pods are allowed to communicate with each other and other network endpoints. Figure 5-2 is a visual representation of how Kubernetes NetworkPolicies control traffic flow between Pods. The diagram shows how policies can be applied to selectively allow or deny communication based on Pod labels, namespaces, and specific protocols or ports. This visual aid will help you understand the concept as we implement a NetworkPolicy using Terraform in the following solution.

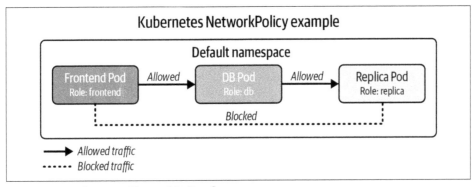

Figure 5-2. Kubernetes NetworkPolicy flow

Solution

You need to apply a Kubernetes NetworkPolicy using Terraform. NetworkPolicies define how groups of Pods are allowed to communicate with each other and other network endpoints:

```
provider "kubernetes" {
  // Configure your Kubernetes provider
}

resource "kubernetes_network_policy" "example" {
  metadata {
    name      = "example"
    namespace = "default"
  }

  spec {
    pod_selector {
      match_labels = {
        "role" = "db"
      }
    }

    policy_types = ["Ingress", "Egress"]

    ingress {
      from {
        pod_selector {
          match_labels = {
            "role" = "frontend"
          }
        }
      }

      ports {
        protocol = "TCP"
        port     = "6379"
      }
    }

    egress {
      to {
        pod_selector {
```

```
        match_labels = {
          "role" = "replica"
        }
      }
    }

    ports {
      protocol = "TCP"
      port     = "6379"
    }
  }
 }
}
```

Discussion

In this solution, we're using the `kubernetes_network_policy` resource to create a
Kubernetes NetworkPolicy:

- The `provider "kubernetes"` block is used to authenticate with the Kubernetes
  cluster. You need to provide the necessary information to connect to your cluster.
- The `resource "kubernetes_network_policy" "example"` block defines a Kuber-
  netes NetworkPolicy:
  — The `metadata` block defines the `name` and `namespace` of the NetworkPolicy.
  — The `spec` block defines the specifications for the NetworkPolicy:
    — `pod_selector` specifies the group of Pods to which the NetworkPolicy
      applies. In this case, it selects Pods with the label `role=db`.
    — `policy_types` specifies the types of traffic to be governed by the policy. It
      can include `"Ingress"`, `"Egress"`, or both.
    — `ingress` specifies the ingress rules. In this case, it allows traffic from Pods
      with the label `role=frontend` on TCP port 6379.
    — `egress` specifies the egress rules. In this case, it allows traffic to Pods with
      the label `role=replica` on TCP port 6379.

This NetworkPolicy allows Pods with the label `role=db` to receive traffic from Pods
with the label `role=frontend` and send traffic to Pods with the label `role=replica`,
both on TCP port 6379. All other inbound and outbound traffic is denied.

It's important to note that NetworkPolicies are additive. If any policy allows a connection, it is allowed. There is no way to deny a particular connection if another policy
allows it.

Also, remember that NetworkPolicies are implemented by the network plug-in, so
you must use a networking solution that supports NetworkPolicy for these to take

effect. Common network plug-ins that support NetworkPolicies include Calico, Cilium, and Weave Net.

When working with NetworkPolicies, consider the following best practices:

- Start with a default deny policy and then add "allow rules" as needed.
- Use namespaces to isolate different environments or applications.
- Label your pods consistently to make policy creation and management easier.
- Regularly review and update your NetworkPolicies as your application architecture evolves.

Always test your NetworkPolicies thoroughly in a nonproduction environment before applying them to your production cluster to ensure they don't unintentionally block necessary traffic.

5.10 Deploying Containers with Helm

Problem

You have to deploy Docker containers on a Kubernetes cluster using Helm charts and Terraform. Helm is a package manager for Kubernetes that simplifies the deployment of applications. Figure 5-3 illustrates the process of Helm chart management in Kubernetes. It shows how Helm charts package Kubernetes resources, how they are stored in repositories, and how they are deployed to Kubernetes clusters. This diagram will help you visualize the workflow we'll be implementing with Terraform in the following solution.

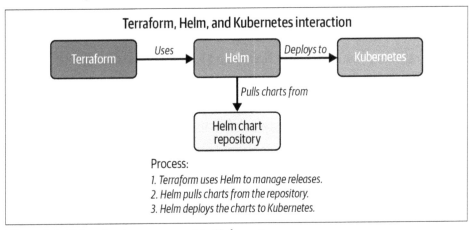

Figure 5-3. Helm chart management in Kubernetes

Solution

Helm charts are the primary way to work with Helm and Kubernetes. Let's explore how we do this in Terraform using a more up-to-date example:

```
provider "helm" {
  kubernetes {
    // Configure your Kubernetes provider
  }
}

resource "helm_release" "example" {
  name       = "my-redis-release"
  repository = "https://charts.bitnami.com/bitnami"
  chart      = "redis"
  version    = "17.3.14"

  set {
    name  = "architecture"
    value = "standalone"
  }

  set {
    name  = "auth.enabled"
    value = "false"
  }
}
```

This example deploys the Redis Helm chart from the Bitnami repository. We're setting it to use a standalone architecture and disabling authentication for simplicity.

Discussion

In this solution, we're using the `helm_release` resource to deploy a Helm chart:

- The `provider "helm"` block is used to configure the Helm provider. It includes a nested `kubernetes` block for configuring the Kubernetes provider. You need to provide the necessary information to connect to your cluster.

- The `resource "helm_release" "example"` block deploys a Helm chart:

  — `name` specifies the name of the Helm release.

  — `repository` specifies the URL of the Helm chart repository. In this case, we're using the Bitnami repository, which is actively maintained.

  — `chart` specifies the name of the Helm chart to deploy.

  — `version` specifies the version of the chart to use. It's a good practice to pin to a specific version for reproducibility.

  — The `set` blocks define values to be passed to the Helm chart. In this example, we're configuring Redis to use a standalone architecture and disabling authentication.

The Helm provider for Terraform provides a convenient way to deploy Helm charts with the benefits of Terraform's state management. You can use it to manage the life cycle of Helm releases and to incorporate Helm releases into your Terraform workflows.

When using Helm with Terraform, consider the following best practices:

- Always specify a chart version to ensure reproducibility.
- Use separate set blocks for each configuration value for clarity.
- For complex configurations, consider using a values file instead of multiple set blocks.
- Be aware of the differences between Helm's upgrade behavior and Terraform's update behavior. Terraform might not be aware of all changes made by Helm.

Remember to replace the repository URL and chart name with the appropriate values for the application you want to deploy. The Bitnami repository is used in this example because it's well-maintained and provides a wide range of applications, but there are many other repositories available depending on your needs.

Finally, always refer to the documentation of the specific Helm chart you're using for the available configuration options and their meanings.

5.11 Enabling Monitoring for Kubernetes Deployments Using Helm

Problem

You need to enable monitoring for your Kubernetes deployments using a monitoring solution such as Prometheus and Grafana, deployed using Helm charts and Terraform. Figure 5-4 provides an overview of how monitoring is implemented in Kubernetes clusters using Prometheus and Grafana, deployed via Terraform. The diagram shows the flow of metrics from Kubernetes resources to Prometheus for collection and storage, and then to Grafana for visualization and alerting. This visual representation will help you understand the monitoring setup we'll be implementing in the following solution.

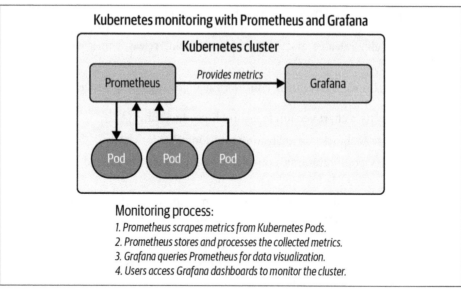

Figure 5-4. Monitoring Kubernetes clusters with Terraform

Solution

This solution will illustrate how to utilize Terraform and Helm to deploy Prometheus and Grafana, enabling robust monitoring for your Kubernetes deployments:

```
provider "helm" {
  kubernetes {
    // Configure your Kubernetes provider
  }
}

resource "helm_release" "prometheus" {
  name       = "prometheus"
  repository = "https://prometheus-community.github.io/helm-charts"
  chart      = "prometheus"
  version    = "15.10.1"  // Specify the desired version

  set {
    name  = "server.persistentVolume.enabled"
    value = "false"  // Disable persistence for simplicity
  }
}

resource "helm_release" "grafana" {
  name       = "grafana"
  repository = "https://grafana.github.io/helm-charts"
  chart      = "grafana"
  version    = "6.43.1"  // Specify the desired version

  set {
    name  = "adminPassword"
    value = "securepassword"  // Replace with a secure password
  }
```

```
set {
  name  = "datasources.datasources\\.yaml.apiVersion"
  value = "1"
}

set {
  name  = "datasources.datasources\\.yaml.datasources[0].name"
  value = "Prometheus"
}

set {
  name  = "datasources.datasources\\.yaml.datasources[0].type"
  value = "prometheus"
}

set {
  name  = "datasources.datasources\\.yaml.datasources[0].url"
  value = "http://prometheus-server"
}

set {
  name  = "datasources.datasources\\.yaml.datasources[0].access"
  value = "proxy"
}
}
```

In this example, Prometheus is deployed from the `prometheus-community` Helm repository, and Grafana is deployed from the `grafana` Helm repository with the admin password set to `admin`.

Discussion

In this solution, we're using the `helm_release` resource to deploy Prometheus and Grafana Helm charts:

- The `provider "helm"` block is used to configure the Helm provider. It includes a nested `kubernetes` block for configuring the Kubernetes provider.
- The `resource "helm_release" "prometheus"` block deploys the Prometheus Helm chart from the `prometheus-community` repository. We're disabling persistent storage for simplicity, but in a production environment, you would typically enable this.
- The `resource "helm_release" "grafana"` block deploys the Grafana Helm chart from the `grafana` repository. We're setting the admin password and configuring a Prometheus data source.

Prometheus is an open source systems monitoring and alerting toolkit. It collects metrics from configured targets at given intervals, evaluates rule expressions, displays the results, and can trigger alerts if some condition is observed to be true.

Grafana is an open source platform for monitoring and observability. It allows you to query, visualize, alert on, and understand your metrics no matter where they are stored. In this setup, Grafana is configured to use Prometheus as its data source.

By deploying Prometheus and Grafana on your Kubernetes cluster, you can monitor your deployments and the state of your cluster. Prometheus will scrape metrics from your deployments, and Grafana will provide a user-friendly interface to visualize these metrics.

Key points to consider:

- Always use specific versions for your Helm charts to ensure reproducibility.
- In a production environment, you should enable persistence for both Prometheus and Grafana to prevent data loss.
- The admin password for Grafana should be managed securely, potentially using Terraform variables or a secrets management solution.
- This is a basic setup. In a real-world scenario, you might need to configure additional settings such as retention periods, resource limits, ingress rules, etc.
- Remember to set up proper access controls and consider the security implications of exposing metrics.

After applying this configuration, you can access Grafana by port-forwarding to the Grafana service and logging in with the admin credentials. From there, you can create dashboards to visualize your Kubernetes metrics collected by Prometheus.

5.12 Scheduling Containers on HashiCorp Nomad

Problem

You need to schedule Docker containers on a HashiCorp Nomad cluster using Terraform. Nomad is a flexible workload orchestrator that can deploy a mix of microservice, batch, containerized, and noncontainerized applications.

Solution

This example demonstrates how to use Terraform to deploy a Docker container running Redis on a Nomad cluster:

```
provider "nomad" {
  address = "http://localhost:4646"
}

resource "nomad_job" "redis" {
  jobspec = file("${path.module}/redis.nomad")
}
```

And here's the content of the redis.nomad file:

```
job "redis" {
  datacenters = ["dc1"]

  group "cache" {
    task "redis" {
      driver = "docker"

      config {
        image = "redis:latest"
        port_map {
          db = 6379
        }
      }

      resources {
        cpu    = 500 # 500 MHz
        memory = 256 # 256MB

        network {
          mbits = 10
          port "db" {}
        }
      }

      service {
        name = "redis"
        port = "db"
        check {
          type     = "tcp"
          interval = "10s"
          timeout  = "2s"
        }
      }
    }
  }
}
```

Discussion

In this solution, we're using the nomad_job resource to deploy a Nomad job that runs a Docker container:

- The provider "nomad" block configures the Nomad provider. You need to specify the address of your Nomad server.
- The resource "nomad_job" "redis" block defines a Nomad job. It uses the file function to read the job specification from an external file (redis.nomad).

The redis.nomad file contains the Nomad job specification:

- The job block defines a job named "redis". A job is the main unit of work in Nomad.
- datacenters specifies the datacenters where the job should be run. In this case, it's set to "dc1".

- The `group` block defines a task group named `"cache"`. A task group is a series of tasks that are colocated on the same Nomad client.

- The `task` block defines a task named `"redis"`:

  — `driver = "docker"` specifies that the Docker driver should be used for this task.

  — The `config` block configures the Docker driver, specifying the image to use and port mapping.

  — The `resources` block specifies the resources required by the task.

  — The `service` block defines a service discovery configuration for the task.

This job specification will schedule a Docker container running Redis on a Nomad client. The Redis service will be registered with the service discovery configuration, and the task will be given the specified resources.

Key points to consider:

- Using an external file for the job specification allows you to use Nomad's HCL syntax, which might be more familiar if you're already using Nomad.

- The `nomad_job` resource in Terraform wraps the job specification and manages its life cycle.

- You can use Terraform variables and functions in your main Terraform configuration to make the job deployment more dynamic.

- Remember that Nomad uses its scheduler, which is different from Kubernetes. Make sure you understand Nomad's architecture and scheduling algorithms when deploying jobs.

- This example doesn't include constraints, update strategies, or other advanced configuration options you might need in a real-world scenario. Refer to the Nomad documentation for a complete list of options.

- Always test your Nomad jobs in a nonproduction environment before deploying to production.

Using Terraform to manage Nomad jobs, you can version control your job specifications and integrate them into your broader IaC workflows.

## CHAPTER 6

HCP Terraform and Terraform Enterprise

This chapter will take a comprehensive journey through HCP Terraform (formerly known as Terraform Cloud) and Terraform Enterprise, exploring their transformative features designed to elevate IaC practices. Whether you're a DevOps engineer, infrastructure manager, or developer looking to scale your IaC practices, this guide will cover everything from setting up your HCP Terraform workspace to managing large-scale deployments.

We'll begin by exploring the setup and configuration of HCP Terraform, then delve into integrating version control systems (VCS) and implementing collaborative workflows. You'll learn how to troubleshoot common issues, enforce policies as code, and effectively manage costs within the HCP Terraform ecosystem. As we progress, we'll examine how to leverage remote operations for scaling deployments and implement advanced state management techniques.

While this chapter focuses primarily on HCP Terraform and Terraform Enterprise, many of the concepts discussed can also be applied to OpenTofu, an open source fork of Terraform. Throughout the chapter, you'll discover how these tools can provide benefits such as centralized state management, enhanced security and compliance, and improved scalability for your infrastructure projects.

By the end of this chapter, you will thoroughly understand how to leverage the capabilities of HCP Terraform, ensuring your infrastructure management processes are as streamlined and effective as possible. Whether you're new to HCP Terraform or looking to optimize your existing setup, the practical recipes in this chapter will significantly equip you with the knowledge to enhance your infrastructure management capabilities.

6.1 Setting Up HCP Terraform

Problem

As teams scale and projects become more complex, managing Terraform states and infrastructure collaboration becomes increasingly challenging.

Solution

HCP Terraform provides a solution by offering a centralized workspace for teams to collaborate on infrastructure projects with secure state management, version control integrations, and automated execution plans. These are the steps to set up HCP Terraform:

1. Create an HCP Terraform account (see Figure 6-1):

    a. Navigate to the HCP Terraform website (*https://oreil.ly/epIkz*).

    b. Sign up for a free account by providing your email and creating a password.

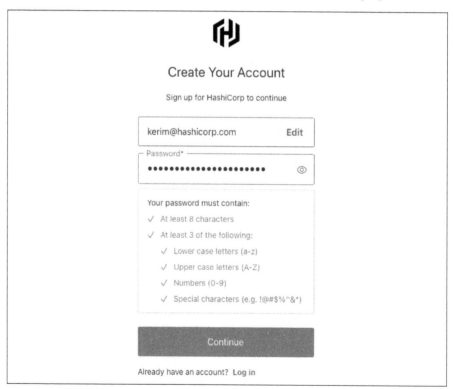

Figure 6-1. HCP Terraform signup page

2. Create an organization (see Figure 6-2):

   a. After logging in, you'll be prompted to create an organization.

   b. Choose a unique name for your organization.

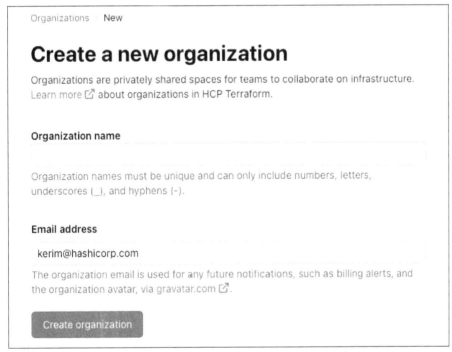

Figure 6-2. Organization creation page

3. Create a new workspace (see Figure 6-3):

   a. In your organization dashboard, click New Workspace.

   b. Choose the type of workflow you want (Version Control Workflow is recommended for most cases).

   c. Connect to your VCS provider (e.g., GitHub, GitLab, Bitbucket).

   d. Select the repository containing your Terraform configuration.

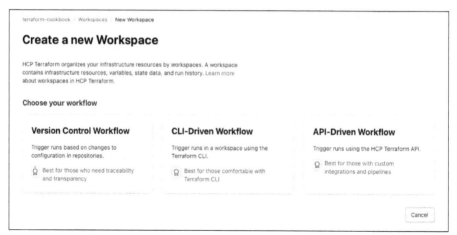

Figure 6-3. Workspace creation process

4. Configure workspace settings (see Figure 6-4):

   a. Set the Terraform working directory if your configuration is not in the repository's root.

   b. Configure environment variables for any sensitive information (such as cloud provider credentials).

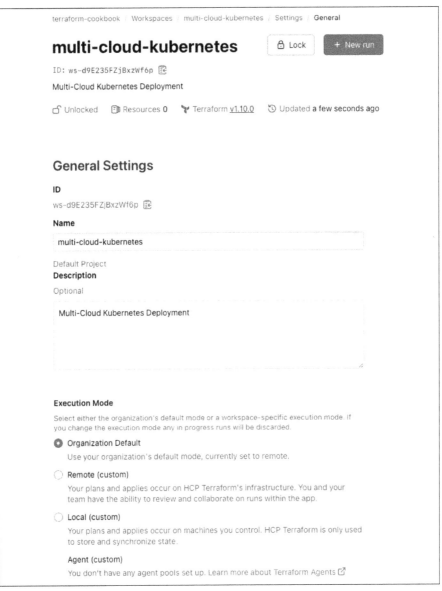

Figure 6-4. Workspace settings page

5. Queue a plan (see Figure 6-5):

   a. Once your workspace is set up, queue your first Terraform plan.

   b. Review the plan output in the HCP Terraform UI.

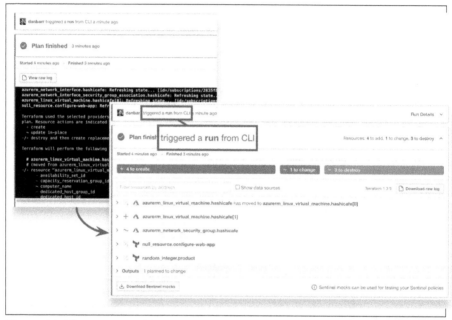

Figure 6-5. Plan output in UI

6. Apply changes. If the plan looks correct, apply the changes to provision your infrastructure.

Discussion

Setting up HCP Terraform is the foundational step toward harnessing its full potential for managing IaC. The process begins with creating an account, which provides access to a user-friendly dashboard for managing workspaces, configurations, and Terraform states.

Creating a workspace linked to a VCS repository is crucial, as it enables automatic plan and application operations triggered by code changes. This automation significantly reduces manual errors and enhances productivity. The workspace is the hub for team collaboration, offering features such as run triggers, workspace variables, and environment settings tailored to streamline the infrastructure management process.

HCP Terraform also simplifies secrets management by securely storing and injecting API tokens, database credentials, and other sensitive information directly into Terraform runs. This feature enhances security by keeping sensitive data out of your code repositories.

Following these initial setup steps, teams can transition to a more collaborative and automated infrastructure workflow. This shift improves efficiency, enhances consistency across environments, and reduces the risk of configuration drift.

Remember, while the initial setup is straightforward, the real power of HCP Terraform comes from how you use it over time. Regularly review and refine your workspace configurations, leverage features such as Sentinel policy checks and cost estimation and encourage your team to fully utilize the collaborative features to get the most out of HCP Terraform.

6.2 Integrating HCP Terraform with VCS

Problem

Integrating HCP Terraform with VCS is essential for automating infrastructure updates and ensuring consistency across environments. However, without a streamlined approach, teams might face manual deployment issues, tracking changes, and collaboration difficulties.

Solution

To integrate Terraform with VCS, such as GitHub, GitLab, or Bitbucket, we will leverage Terraform's native support for VCS providers within HCP Terraform and Terraform Enterprise. This approach ensures a seamless workflow, where IaC changes are automatically applied following code commits and merges.

Here's a step-by-step guide to set up VCS integration:

1. Configure the HCP Terraform backend in your Terraform configuration:

```
terraform {
  cloud {
    organization = "<your-organization-name>"

    workspaces {
      name = "<your-workspace-name>"
    }
  }
}
```

2. In the HCP Terraform UI, navigate to your workspace settings and select Version Control.

3. Choose your VCS provider (e.g., GitHub) and follow the prompts to authenticate and authorize HCP Terraform.

4. Select the repository containing your Terraform configurations.

5. Configure any additional settings, such as the branch to use and subdirectory if your Terraform files are not in the repository's root.

6. Save the VCS settings.

When changes are pushed to the connected repository, HCP Terraform will automatically trigger a plan. If auto-apply is enabled, it will also apply the changes after a successful plan.

Discussion

This solution outlines a basic setup for integrating Terraform with a VCS provider. Here are some key points to consider:

Configuring HCP Terraform or Terraform Enterprise
Using HCP Terraform as the backend provides advanced features for state management, collaboration, and CI/CD integration. Ensure your Terraform configurations are connected to a workspace in HCP Terraform.

Connecting to a VCS provider
HCP Terraform supports various VCS providers. This connection is authenticated via tokens, facilitating operations such as repository management, team collaboration, and more within Terraform configurations.

Managing VCS resources
With the VCS provider configured, you can now manage resources like repositories, branches, and permissions as part of your IaC. This approach centralizes infrastructure and codebase management, streamlining operations and ensuring consistency across environments.

Workflow automation
By integrating with VCS, you enable a GitOps workflow where infrastructure changes are applied through pull requests and code reviews. This enhances collaboration and ensures best practices in infrastructure management.

Security considerations
When integrating with VCS, ensure that sensitive information (such as API keys or passwords) is never committed to the repository. Instead, use HCP Terraform variable management features to securely store and use these sensitive values.

Branch strategies

Consider implementing branch protection rules in your VCS to require pull request reviews before merging changes to main branches. This adds an extra layer of security and quality control to your infrastructure changes.

Adjust the configurations to match your specific VCS provider and organizational structure. This integration enables automated workflows where infrastructure changes are applied through pull requests and code reviews, enhancing collaboration and ensuring best practices in infrastructure management.

Remember to regularly review and update your VCS integration settings as your project evolves. This will help maintain the security and efficiency of your infrastructure management process.

6.3 Consuming Terraform State with HCP Terraform

Problem

Managing and sharing Terraform state files can be challenging in Terraform projects, especially those involving multiple environments or team collaboration.

Solution

To use HCP Terraform for state management, configure your Terraform configuration file with a cloud block:

```
terraform {
  cloud {
    organization = "example-org"  # Replace with your organization name
    workspaces {
      name = "example-workspace"  # Replace with your workspace name
    }
  }
}

# Example resource (not required for state management setup)
resource "aws_instance" "example" {
  ami           = "ami-123456"  # Replace with a valid AMI ID
  instance_type = "t2.micro"
}
```

Discussion

The solution leverages HCP Terraform as a remote backend for managing Terraform state files. This approach provides several benefits:

Centralized state management

HCP Terraform provides a secure, centralized location for storing state files, facilitating easy access and collaboration among team members.

State locking
> HCP Terraform automatically implements state locking, preventing concurrent operations that could corrupt your state.

Version control
> HCP Terraform maintains a history of your state files, allowing you to review changes over time and revert if necessary.

Access control
> You can manage who has access to your state files through HCP Terraform built-in access controls.

Operational consistency
> By using HCP Terraform, you ensure that all team members are working with the same, up-to-date state information.

Reduced risk
> Storing state remotely reduces the risk of losing state files or accidentally committing sensitive information to version control.

When using this setup, keep in mind:

- Ensure all team members have the necessary permissions in HCP Terraform to access the state.
- Be cautious when sharing workspace names or organization names publicly, as they could potentially be used to infer information about your infrastructure.
- Regularly review your HCP Terraform settings and access logs to maintain security.

By addressing the problem with a HCP Terraform remote backend, you can streamline your Terraform workflows, enhance security, and improve collaboration across your team. This approach is particularly beneficial for larger teams or more complex infrastructure setups where coordinating state becomes challenging.

6.4 Using HCP Terraform with GitHub Actions

Problem

Teams often seek to automate their infrastructure management workflows by integrating Terraform with CI/CD tools such as GitHub Actions. The challenge is establishing a seamless automation pipeline that can handle Terraform plans and apply operations securely and efficiently upon code changes in a GitHub repository.

Solution

Create a workflow file in your repository to automate Terraform operations through GitHub Actions. Here's an example of a GitHub Actions workflow that integrates with HCP Terraform:

```
name: 'Terraform GitHub Actions'

on:
  push:
    branches:
    - main

jobs:
  terraform:
    name: 'Terraform'
    runs-on: ubuntu-latest
    steps:
    - name: Checkout
      uses: actions/checkout@v4

    - name: Setup Terraform
      uses: hashicorp/setup-terraform@v1
      with:
        terraform_version: 1.10.0
        cli_config_credentials_token: ${{ secrets.TF_API_TOKEN }}

    - name: Terraform Init
      run: terraform init

    - name: Terraform Format
      run: terraform fmt -check -recursive

    - name: Terraform Plan
      run: terraform plan

    - name: Terraform Apply
      run: terraform apply -auto-approve
      if: github.ref == 'refs/heads/main'
```

This workflow automates Terraform operations on pushes to the main branch, using an HCP Terraform API token for authentication.

Discussion

The provided GitHub Actions workflow automates Terraform operations, integrating tightly with HCP Terraform for enhanced state management and operational efficiency. Here's a breakdown of the key components:

Workflow trigger
> The workflow is configured to trigger on push events to the main branch, ensuring that Terraform operations are automatically initiated following code changes.

Checkout step
> This step checks out the repository content into the GitHub Actions runner, making the Terraform configurations available for subsequent steps.

`Setup Terraform` *step*

> This action prepares the GitHub Actions environment with the specified Terraform version and configures the Terraform CLI with credentials for HCP Terraform, enabling authenticated interactions.

`Terraform Init`

> Initializes the Terraform working directory, preparing the backend and downloading necessary plug-ins.

`Terraform Format`

> Verifies that the Terraform files are correctly formatted, acting as a quality check.

`Terraform Plan`

> Creates an execution plan, allowing for review of the proposed changes.

`Terraform Apply`

> Applies the changes specified by the Terraform plan. The condition ensures that `terraform apply` is executed only on the main branch.

Key considerations for this setup include:

- Securely store the `TF_API_TOKEN` in GitHub Secrets to authenticate with HCP Terraform.
- The `-auto-approve` flag in the apply step automatically applies the plan without manual intervention. Use this with caution, especially in production environments.
- Consider adding manual approval steps or using pull request workflows for more controlled deployments.
- Adjust the workflow to match your branching strategy and deployment process.

This integration enables a GitOps approach where infrastructure changes are automatically applied through code commits, enhancing collaboration and ensuring consistency in infrastructure management.

6.5 Collaborative Workflows with HCP Terraform

Problem

Enabling collaborative workflows when using HCP Terraform is essential for teams to work together efficiently on Terraform projects. Teams require a structured approach to managing IaC that supports version control, code review, and automated deployments in a consistent and scalable manner.

Solution

To facilitate collaborative workflows with HCP Terraform, follow these steps:

1. Set up workspaces:

```
# In your Terraform configuration
terraform {
  cloud {
    organization = "your-org-name"

    workspaces {
      name = "project-environment"  # e.g., "production" or "staging"
    }
  }
}
```

2. Version control integration:

   a. In HCP Terraform, navigate to your workspace settings.

   b. Under Version Control, connect to your VCS provider (e.g., GitHub).

   c. Select the repository containing your Terraform configurations.

3. Configure workspace variables. In the workspace settings, add environment variables for sensitive data:

```
AWS_ACCESS_KEY_ID     = <your-access-key>
AWS_SECRET_ACCESS_KEY = <your-secret-key>
```

4. Set up team access:

   a. In your HCP Terraform organization settings, create teams and assign permissions.

   b. Add team members and grant access to specific workspaces.

5. Implement a pull request workflow:

   a. Create feature branches for changes.

   b. Open pull requests for review before merging to main.

Discussion

Utilizing HCP Terraform for collaborative workflows enhances security and efficiency in managing infrastructure. Here's a deeper look at the key aspects:

Workspaces
   Provide logical separation of environments, making it easier to manage complex infrastructure across different stages of development. Each workspace can have its own variables, state, and access controls.

Version control integration

Ensures that all infrastructure changes are versioned and undergo a review process. This reduces the likelihood of errors and provides an audit trail of changes.

Workspace variables

Securely store sensitive information such as API keys and access tokens. These variables are injected at runtime, keeping your Terraform code clean and secure.

Team access and RBAC

Ensures that only authorized personnel can make or approve changes to the infrastructure, enhancing security and compliance. Different teams can be given varying levels of access based on their roles.

Pull request workflow

Encourages code review and collaboration before changes are applied. This can be further enhanced with HCP Terraform speculative plans on pull requests, allowing team members to see the potential impact of changes before they're merged.

Additional benefits include:

Automated runs

Reduce manual errors and save time by automating the execution of Terraform commands.

State management

HCP Terraform provides a centralized and secure location for state files, eliminating the need to manage state locally or in separate storage systems.

Run triggers

Allow you to create dependencies between workspaces, ensuring that changes in one part of your infrastructure trigger appropriate updates in dependent parts.

By incorporating these practices, teams can achieve a more structured, secure, and collaborative approach to infrastructure management, leveraging the full power of IaC for scalable and efficient operations.

6.6 Troubleshooting HCP Terraform and Terraform Enterprise

Problem

Teams utilizing HCP Terraform or Terraform Enterprise may encounter issues or unexpected behavior during infrastructure management tasks. These problems range from configuration errors and authentication issues to integration mishaps with VCS.

Solution

To troubleshoot issues in HCP Terraform and Terraform Enterprise, follow these steps:

1. Review Terraform runs:

    ```
    # In HCP Terraform UI
    Navigate to the specific run > View "Details" tab
    Check VCS integration:
    # In HCP Terraform UI
    Workspace Settings > Version Control > Verify connection status
    ```

2. Examine workspace configuration:

    ```
    # In HCP Terraform UI
    Workspace Settings > General Settings
    Workspace Settings > Variables
    ```

3. Validate Terraform configuration:

    ```
    # Locally
    terraform init
    terraform validate
    ```

4. Inspect authentication and permissions:

    ```
    # In HCP Terraform UI
    Organization Settings > Teams > Review member permissions
    Workspace Settings > Variables > Check for credential variables
    ```

5. Use Sentinel policies:

    ```
    # Example Sentinel policy
    main = rule {
      all tfplan.resources.aws_instance as _, instances {
        all instances as _, r {
          r.applied.instance_type is "t2.micro"
        }
      }
    }
    ```

6. Check HCP Terraform status:

    ```
    Visit: https://status.hashicorp.com/
    ```

Discussion

Effective troubleshooting in HCP Terraform and Terraform Enterprise requires a systematic approach:

Reviewing Terraform runs
Examine the logs of failed Terraform runs. HCP Terraform provides detailed logs for each Terraform life cycle operation, which can often pinpoint the source of the issue.

Checking VCS integration
> Verify the VCS integration settings if the problem is related to triggering runs from VCS. Ensure that webhooks are correctly configured and that HCP Terraform has the necessary permissions to access the repositories.

Examining workspace configuration
> Misconfiguration in workspace settings can lead to unexpected behavior. Review the workspace configuration, including environment variables, Terraform version, and any overridden settings.

Validating Terraform configuration
> Errors in Terraform configurations can cause failures. Use `terraform validate` locally to check for syntax errors or misconfigurations in your Terraform files.

Inspecting authentication and permissions
> Verify that the correct credentials are stored as environment variables in HCP Terraform workspaces for issues related to accessing external resources or providers. Ensure these credentials have appropriate permissions.

Using Sentinel policies
> If you encounter unexpected blocks or behaviors in Terraform runs due to policy checks, review the Sentinel policies applied to your organization or workspaces. Ensure that policies are correctly written and align with your infrastructure goals.

Checking HCP Terraform status
> Sometimes, issues may be due to outages or maintenance in HCP Terraform itself. Check the HCP Terraform status page for any ongoing incidents that might be affecting your operations.

Remember to consult the Terraform documentation and community forums for additional insights. For unresolved issues, especially those that might be bugs or require deeper insights into HCP Terraform operations, contact HashiCorp support for assistance.

By systematically reviewing each aspect of your Terraform setup, from configurations and workspace settings to external integrations and permissions, you can identify and resolve issues more efficiently. Keeping your Terraform versions up to date and following best practices for infrastructure as code can also help in minimizing troubleshooting needs.

6.7 Enforcing Policy as Code

Problem

As teams scale their infrastructure with Terraform, managing and enforcing compliance, security, and operational standards becomes increasingly complex. The challenge lies in ensuring that all deployed resources meet the organization's policies without introducing significant manual oversight or hindering the pace of development.

Solution

HCP Terraform and Terraform Enterprise offer Sentinel, a policy-as-code framework, to define and enforce policies. Here's an example of implementing a Sentinel policy:

```
# This policy ensures all EC2 instances are t2.micro
import "tfplan"

ec2_instance_type = rule {
    all tfplan.resources.aws_instance as _, instances {
        all instances as _, r {
            r.applied.instance_type is "t2.micro"
        }
    }
}
main = rule {
    ec2_instance_type
}
```

1. Create a Sentinel policy file (e.g., *restrict-instance-type.sentinel*).

2. In HCP Terraform, navigate to your organization settings and create a policy set:

    a. Go to Settings → Policy Sets.

    b. Click "Connect a new policy set."

    c. Choose your VCS provider and select the repository containing your Sentinel policies.

    d. Configure the policy set to apply to relevant workspaces.

3. Apply the policy to your Terraform runs:

    a. The policy will automatically be evaluated during Terraform plans and applies.

    b. If a policy check fails, the run will be halted, and details of the violation will be provided.

Discussion

Implementing policy as code with Sentinel in HCP Terraform and Terraform Enterprise centralizes and automates compliance and governance across your infrastructure. This approach offers several benefits:

Automated enforcement
    Policies are automatically checked on every Terraform run, ensuring consistent application of standards without manual intervention.

Flexibility

Sentinel's policy language allows for complex, fine-grained control over your infrastructure. You can enforce a wide range of policies, from security rules to cost management guidelines.

Version control

Policies can be stored in version control systems, allowing for change tracking, peer review, and rollback capabilities.

Customization

Policies can be tailored to your organization's specific needs, allowing you to enforce both industry-standard best practices and internal guidelines.

Integrated workflow

Policy checks become an integral part of the infrastructure deployment process, catching potential issues early in the development cycle.

Auditing and compliance

With policies defined as code, it's easier to demonstrate compliance with various regulatory standards and internal policies.

When implementing policy as code:

- Start with simple policies and gradually increase complexity as your team becomes more familiar with Sentinel.
- Regularly review and update policies to ensure they remain relevant and effective.
- Use policy sets to group related policies and apply them to relevant workspaces.
- Consider implementing soft-mandatory policies that can be overridden with appropriate approvals for exceptional cases.

By incorporating policy as code into your Terraform workflows, you can ensure that your infrastructure meets your technical and operational requirements while aligning with your organization's standards and best practices.

6.8 Managing Costs with HCP Terraform

Problem

Managing and optimizing costs in cloud computing is a critical concern for businesses. As teams deploy and scale their infrastructure using HCP Terraform, it becomes essential to have mechanisms in place to monitor, control, and optimize cloud spending.

Solution

HCP Terraform offers several features to assist in managing costs. Here's a set of configurations and policies that demonstrate how to leverage these features:

```
# Enable cost estimation in your HCP Terraform workspace
terraform {
  cloud {
    organization = "your-organization"

    workspaces {
      name = "your-workspace"
    }
  }
}

# Sentinel policy for cost control (limit-monthly-cost.sentinel)
import "tfrun"
import "decimal"

monthly_cost_limit = decimal.new(1000)

main = rule {
    decimal.less_than(tfrun.cost_estimate.delta_monthly_cost, monthly_cost_limit)
}

# Set up a notification for cost alerts
resource "tfe_notification_configuration" "cost_alert" {
  name             = "Cost Alert"
  destination_type = "email"
  email_user_ids   = ["user1", "user2"]
  triggers         = ["cost_estimation_completed"]
  workspace_id     = tfe_workspace.example.id
}

# Use Terraform modules to standardize resource configurations
module "ec2_instance" {
  source  = "terraform-aws-modules/ec2-instance/aws"
  version = "~> 3.0"

  name = "cost-optimized-instance"

  instance_type         = "t3.micro"
  monitoring            = true
  vpc_security_group_ids = ["sg-12345678"]
  subnet_id             = "subnet-eddcdzz4"

  tags = {
    Environment = "dev"
    Project     = "cost-optimization"
  }
}
```

To implement these cost management features:

1. Enable cost estimation in your HCP Terraform workspace settings.

2. Create and apply the Sentinel policy in your HCP Terraform organization's policy sets.

3. Configure the notification setting in your HCP Terraform workspace.

4. Implement standardized, cost-optimized modules in your Terraform configurations.

5. Regularly review cost estimates and alerts to optimize your infrastructure spending.

Discussion

Managing costs in HCP Terraform involves several key strategies:

Cost estimation
HCP Terraform cost estimation feature provides an overview of the potential costs associated with a Terraform plan before it's applied. This allows teams to assess the financial impact of their changes upfront.

Sentinel policies
Utilize Sentinel, Terraform's policy-as-code framework, to enforce cost-control policies. These policies can limit resource sizes, types, or even total cost per deployment.

Notifications
While HCP Terraform doesn't directly send budget alerts, you can set up notifications for cost estimation events. This helps teams stay informed about potential cost impacts of their infrastructure changes.

Workspace organization
Efficiently organize workspaces to separate different environments, projects, or teams. This organizational strategy, combined with cost estimation and policies, simplifies managing costs by providing clearer visibility into where costs are incurred.

Terraform modules
Leverage reusable Terraform modules to standardize resource provisioning across your organization. Modules can be designed to include cost-efficient resource configurations.

Regular review and refactoring
Regularly review your Terraform configurations and cloud resource utilization. Look for opportunities to refactor or downsize resources based on actual usage metrics.

By embedding these cost management practices into your Terraform workflows, you can ensure that your cloud infrastructure not only meets your technical and operational requirements but also aligns with your financial goals. This approach helps in balancing innovation, performance, and cost-efficiency in your infrastructure management.

Remember to regularly update your cost management strategies as cloud provider pricing models and your infrastructure needs evolve. Combining these HCP Terraform features with your cloud provider's native cost management tools can provide a comprehensive approach to managing and optimizing your cloud spending.

6.9 Utilizing Remote Operations for Large-Scale Deployments

Problem

When managing large-scale deployments with Terraform, teams often encounter challenges related to performance, resource constraints, and operational complexities. These challenges can include long execution times for Terraform plans and applies, limited resources on local machines, and the need for centralized logging and state management.

Solution

HCP Terraform offers remote operations as a solution to these challenges, providing a way to execute Terraform plans and applies on HashiCorp's infrastructure. Here's a configuration that demonstrates how to set up and use remote operations in HCP Terraform:

```
# Configure HCP Terraform workspace for remote operations
terraform {
  cloud {
    organization = "your-organization"

    workspaces {
      name = "large-scale-deployment"
    }
  }
}

# Example of a large-scale deployment resource
resource "aws_vpc" "main" {
  cidr_block = "10.0.0.0/16"

  tags = {
    Name = "Large Scale VPC"
    Environment = "Production"
  }
}

# Use of a module for standardized deployments
module "ec2_cluster" {
  source  = "terraform-aws-modules/ec2-instance/aws"
  version = "~> 3.0"

  for_each = toset(["1", "2", "3", "4", "5"])

  name = "instance-${each.key}"
```

```
ami                     = "ami-ebd02392"
instance_type           = "t3.micro"
key_name                = "user1"
monitoring              = true
vpc_security_group_ids  = ["sg-12345678"]
subnet_id               = "subnet-eddcdzz4"

  tags = {
    Environment = "Production"
    Terraform   = "true"
  }
}

# Sentinel policy to enforce resource tagging (in a separate .sentinel file)
import "tfplan"

required_tags = ["Environment", "Project"]

main = rule {
  all tfplan.resources as _, instances {
    all instances as _, r {
      all required_tags as t {
        r.applied.tags contains t
      }
    }
  }
}
```

To utilize remote operations for large-scale deployments:

1. Set up an HCP Terraform workspace with remote execution mode enabled.

2. Configure your Terraform code to use the HCP Terraform backend, as shown in the example.

3. Set up any necessary environment variables and Terraform variables in the HCP Terraform workspace settings.

4. Implement Sentinel policies to enforce standards across your large-scale deployment.

5. Use the HCP Terraform UI or API to trigger runs or configure VCS integration for automatic runs on code changes.

6. Monitor the progress of your runs in the HCP Terraform UI, where you can view logs, approve plans, and manage state.

7. Utilize HCP Terraform's state management features for collaboration and tracking changes across your team.

Discussion

Remote operations in HCP Terraform provide several benefits for managing large-scale deployments:

Scalability

By offloading resource-intensive operations to HCP Terraform, teams can run larger deployments without being limited by their local machine's resources.

Centralized state management

HCP Terraform provides a centralized and secure location for storing state files, eliminating the need to manage state locally or in separate storage systems.

Collaboration

The centralized nature of HCP Terraform enhances collaboration among team members, as operations are accessible through the HCP Terraform UI.

Version control integration

Integrating with VCS ensures that deployments are consistent, compliant, and streamlined, reducing manual errors and operational overhead.

Policy enforcement

Implementing policy as code through Sentinel ensures that deployments are consistent and compliant across your entire infrastructure.

Visibility and auditing

HCP Terraform provides detailed logs and a history of all operations, improving visibility and making it easier to audit changes.

Concurrent operations

HCP Terraform can manage multiple concurrent operations, which is particularly useful for large-scale deployments with interdependent components.

When utilizing remote operations, it's important to structure your Terraform configurations and workspaces efficiently. Proper organization and modularization of Terraform code facilitate better management and scalability of large infrastructures.

By leveraging these features, teams can manage large-scale deployments more effectively, ensuring consistent, secure, and cost-efficient infrastructure provisioning across complex environments.

6.10 Advanced State Management and Recovery

Problem

Managing state files can become challenging in complex Terraform projects, particularly as infrastructure grows in scale and complexity. Issues like state lock conflicts, state drift, and the need for state recovery after unintended modifications or deletions are common.

Solution

HCP Terraform offers advanced state management and recovery features to handle complex state-related scenarios efficiently. Here's an example of how to configure and use these features:

```
# Configure HCP Terraform backend
terraform {
  cloud {
    organization = "<your-organization>"

    workspaces {
      name = "advanced-state-management"
    }
  }
}

# Example resource to demonstrate state management
resource "aws_s3_bucket" "example" {
  bucket = "my-tf-test-bucket"
  acl    = "private"

  tags = {
    Name        = "My bucket"
    Environment = "Dev"
  }
}

# Sentinel policy for state enforcement (in a separate .sentinel file)
import "tfstate"

main = rule {
  all tfstate.resources.aws_s3_bucket as _, buckets {
    all buckets as _, bucket {
      bucket.attr.acl is "private"
    }
  }
}
```

To utilize advanced state management and recovery features in HCP Terraform:

1. Configure your Terraform configuration to use HCP Terraform as the backend.

2. Enable state locking in your HCP Terraform workspace settings to prevent concurrent executions.

3. Implement Sentinel policies to enforce constraints on state files.

4. Use the HCP Terraform UI or API to inspect current state and identify discrepancies.

5. To recover a previous state version:

   a. Navigate to the States tab in your HCP Terraform workspace.

   b. Select the desired state version.

   c. Click Restore to revert to that state.

6. For manual state manipulations (use cautiously):

a. Use `terraform state` commands locally with appropriate credentials.

b. Example: `terraform state rm aws_s3_bucket.example`.

Discussion

Advanced state management in HCP Terraform provides several benefits for complex infrastructure management:

State locking
Prevents concurrent executions that could lead to state corruption.

State history and versioning
Maintains a detailed history of state changes, allowing teams to track modifications over time and restore previous versions if needed.

State recovery
Allows to restore previous state versions in case of unintended alterations or deletions.

Sentinel policies for state enforcement
Helps enforce constraints on state files, ensuring all changes meet organizational standards and compliance requirements.

State inspections
Facilitates the identification of discrepancies between desired and actual infrastructure configuration.

Workspace variables for state isolation
Enables isolation of state files across different environments, minimizing the risk of cross-environment state contamination.

When using these features, it's important to:

- Use automated and built-in HCP Terraform mechanisms, which are preferred over manual state manipulations.
- Use caution with manual state operations and ensure all team members are informed about changes.
- Regularly review and audit state changes to maintain infrastructure integrity.
- Implement a robust backup strategy for your Terraform configurations and state files.

By leveraging these advanced state management capabilities, teams can significantly enhance their infrastructure's safety, compliance, and manageability as code practices, especially in large-scale and complex cloud environments.

## CHAPTER 7

Consuming and Managing Secrets with Terraform

In the world of infrastructure as code, managing secrets is critical to maintaining the security and integrity of your systems. Secrets, such as API keys, database passwords, and other sensitive information, require careful handling to prevent unauthorized access and potential breaches. Terraform provides various mechanisms for securely consuming and managing secrets within your infrastructure deployments.

One key challenge with secrets management is striking the right balance between security and accessibility. Terraform offers a range of options to address this challenge, including using encrypted backends, external secret management systems, and secure input variables. By leveraging these approaches, you can ensure that secrets are properly encrypted, stored securely, and accessed only by authorized entities.

This chapter explores the best practices and techniques for handling secrets in Terraform. We'll cover different approaches to securely storing, consuming, and managing secrets, ensuring your infrastructure remains protected and compliant with security standards.

As we progress through the chapter, we'll also explore best practices for managing secrets in collaborative environments, such as using version control systems and implementing proper access controls. We'll discuss strategies for rotating and updating secrets, ensuring your infrastructure remains secure over time.

By the end of this chapter, you'll have a solid understanding of how to consume and manage secrets effectively in Terraform. You'll be able to apply these techniques to your infrastructure deployments, enhancing the security posture of your systems and protecting sensitive information from unauthorized access.

7.1 Dealing with Sensitive Data in Terraform

Problem

When working with Terraform, you often need to manage sensitive data such as passwords, API keys, or certificates. Storing this sensitive information directly in your Terraform configuration files is not recommended, as it poses security risks. How can you securely handle sensitive data in Terraform while keeping it out of your configuration files?

Solution

To handle sensitive data securely in Terraform, you can use a combination of AWS Secrets Manager and Terraform variables. This approach keeps your sensitive data out of your Terraform configuration files and allows for secure retrieval during Terraform operations:

```
# Configure the AWS provider
provider "aws" {
  region = "us-west-2"
}

# Retrieve the secret from AWS Secrets Manager
data "aws_secretsmanager_secret" "db_password" {
  name = "prod/db/password"
}

data "aws_secretsmanager_secret_version" "db_password" {
  secret_id = data.aws_secretsmanager_secret.db_password.id
}

# Define a variable for the sensitive data
variable "db_password" {
  type        = string
  description = "Database password"
  sensitive   = true
}

# Use the retrieved secret in your resource configuration
resource "aws_db_instance" "example" {
  # ... other configuration ...
  password = jsondecode(data.aws_secretsmanager_secret_version.db_password.secret_string)["password"]
}

# Output the DB endpoint (non-sensitive data)
output "db_endpoint" {
  value = aws_db_instance.example.endpoint
}
```

Discussion

In this solution, we use AWS Secrets Manager to store and retrieve sensitive data, keeping it out of our Terraform configuration files. Here's a breakdown of the approach:

---

1. We configure the AWS provider to interact with AWS services.

2. We use the `aws_secretsmanager_secret` and `aws_secretsmanager_secret_version` data sources to retrieve the secret from AWS Secrets Manager. The secret is identified by its name in Secrets Manager.

3. We define a variable `db_password` with the `sensitive = true` attribute. This ensures that Terraform treats this variable as sensitive and doesn't display its value in logs or output.

4. In the `aws_db_instance` resource, we use the retrieved secret to set the database password. We use `jsondecode` to parse the JSON-formatted secret string and extract the password value.

5. We include an output for the database endpoint. Note that we only output nonsensitive information.

This approach offers several benefits:

- Sensitive data is stored securely in AWS Secrets Manager, not in Terraform files.
- The `sensitive = true` attribute on the variable prevents accidental exposure of the secret in Terraform output.
- Secrets can be rotated in AWS Secrets Manager without changing Terraform code.
- Access to secrets can be controlled using AWS IAM policies.

When using this method, ensure that:

- Your AWS credentials have the necessary permissions to access Secrets Manager.
- You follow AWS best practices for securing access to Secrets Manager.
- You don't accidentally log or output the sensitive values in your Terraform configuration.

By using a secrets management service like AWS Secrets Manager in combination with Terraform's sensitive variables, you can maintain the security of your sensitive data while still being able to use it in your Terraform configurations.

7.2 Retrieving Key-Values from HashiCorp Vault

Problem

When working with sensitive data in Terraform, it's often necessary to retrieve key-value pairs from HashiCorp Vault. Vault provides a secure way to store and manage secrets, and Terraform can integrate with Vault to retrieve these secrets during the provisioning process.

Solution

To retrieve key-value pairs from HashiCorp Vault in Terraform, you can use the Vault provider and the `vault_generic_secret` data source:

```
# Configure the Vault provider
provider "vault" {
  address = "https://vault.example.com"
}

# Retrieve key-value pairs from Vault
data "vault_generic_secret" "example" {
  path = "secret/example"
}

# Use the retrieved key-value pairs in your resource configuration
resource "example_resource" "example" {
  # ... other configuration ...
  username = data.vault_generic_secret.example.data["username"]
  password = data.vault_generic_secret.example.data["password"]
}
```

Discussion

In this solution, we integrate Terraform with HashiCorp Vault to securely retrieve and use secrets. Here's a breakdown of the approach:

1. We configure the Vault provider with the address of our Vault server. Note that we've removed the explicit `token` attribute from the provider configuration.

2. We use the `vault_generic_secret` data source to retrieve the secret from Vault. The `path` attribute specifies the path in Vault where the key-value pairs are stored.

3. The retrieved key-value pairs are accessible through the `data` attribute of the data source. We can access individual key-value pairs using the syntax `data.vault_generic_secret.example.data["key"]`.

4. In the resource configuration, we use the retrieved secrets by referencing the appropriate keys from the Vault data source.

This approach offers several benefits:

- Secrets are stored securely in Vault, not in Terraform files or version control.
- Vault provides advanced features like dynamic secrets, secret rotation, and fine-grained access control.
- Secrets can be rotated or updated in Vault without changing Terraform code.

When using this method, consider the following best practices:

- Use Vault's authentication methods instead of hard-coding tokens. For example, if Terraform runs in AWS, you might use the AWS auth method.
- If running Terraform locally or in an environment without a native Vault auth method, consider using Vault's AppRole auth method before using Vault tokens.
- Set up appropriate Vault policies to control access to secrets.
- Ensure secure communication between Terraform and Vault, preferably using Transport Layer Security (TLS).
- Regularly audit access to secrets in Vault.

By leveraging HashiCorp Vault and Terraform's integration with Vault, you can securely manage and retrieve sensitive key-value pairs in your infrastructure provisioning process. This approach provides a robust and flexible solution for handling secrets in your Terraform deployments.

7.3 Managing Kubernetes Secrets with Kubernetes-Native Functions

Problem

When working with Kubernetes and Terraform, you may need to manage sensitive data as Kubernetes Secrets. Kubernetes provides native functions to create and manage Secrets within a cluster. How can we use Kubernetes-native functions in Terraform to manage Kubernetes Secrets securely?

Solution

To manage Kubernetes Secrets using Kubernetes-native functions in Terraform, you can use the Kubernetes provider and the kubernetes_secret resource:

```
# Configure the Kubernetes provider
provider "kubernetes" {
  config_path = "~/.kube/config"
}

# Define variables for sensitive data
variable "database_username" {
  type        = string
  description = "Database username"
  sensitive   = true
}

variable "database_password" {
  type        = string
  description = "Database password"
  sensitive   = true
```

```
}

# Create a Kubernetes Secret
resource "kubernetes_secret" "example_secret" {
  metadata {
    name = "example-secret"
  }

  data = {
    username = var.database_username
    password = var.database_password
  }
}

# Use the Kubernetes Secret in a Pod configuration
resource "kubernetes_pod" "example_pod" {
  metadata {
    name = "example-pod"
  }

  spec {
    container {
      name  = "example-container"
      image = "example-image"

      env {
        name = "DATABASE_USERNAME"
        value_from {
          secret_key_ref {
            name = kubernetes_secret.example_secret.metadata[0].name
            key  = "username"
          }
        }
      }

      env {
        name = "DATABASE_PASSWORD"
        value_from {
          secret_key_ref {
            name = kubernetes_secret.example_secret.metadata[0].name
            key  = "password"
          }
        }
      }
    }
  }
}
```

Discussion

In this solution, we use Terraform to create and manage Kubernetes Secrets, and
then use those Secrets in a Kubernetes Pod configuration. Here's a breakdown of the
approach:

1. We configure the Kubernetes provider with the path to the Kubernetes configuration file.

2. We define variables for the sensitive data (database username and password) with
   the sensitive = true attribute to ensure Terraform handles them securely.

---

3. We use the `kubernetes_secret` resource to create a Kubernetes Secret. The secret data is populated using the variables we defined.

4. We create a Kubernetes Pod using the `kubernetes_pod` resource. Within the Pod specification, we reference the Secret we created to set environment variables.

5. The Secret values are securely passed to the container's environment variables using the `value_from` block with the `secret_key_ref` attribute.

This approach offers several benefits:

- Sensitive data is stored as Kubernetes Secrets, leveraging Kubernetes' built-in secret management capabilities.
- Secrets are not stored in plain text in Terraform files or version control.
- Kubernetes handles the encryption of Secrets at rest (when configured properly).
- Access to Secrets can be controlled using Kubernetes RBAC policies.

When using this method, consider the following best practices:

- Ensure your Kubernetes cluster is configured to encrypt Secrets at rest.
- Use Kubernetes RBAC to control access to Secrets.
- Avoid outputting Secret values in Terraform.
- Consider using external secret management systems (like HashiCorp Vault) with Kubernetes Secrets for additional security features.
- Regularly rotate Secrets and update the Terraform configuration accordingly.

By using Kubernetes-native functions for managing Secrets, you can ensure that your sensitive data is handled securely within your Kubernetes deployments managed by Terraform. This approach provides a native and integrated solution for secret management in Kubernetes environments.

7.4 Managing Kubernetes Secrets with Vault and Terraform

Problem

When working with Kubernetes and Terraform, you may want to utilize HashiCorp Vault as a secure secrets management solution. Vault provides advanced features for storing and managing sensitive data, and it can be integrated with Kubernetes to inject secrets into Pods securely. This integration allows for centralized secrets management and enhanced security features. Figure 7-1 illustrates this complex interaction, showing how Terraform, Vault, and Kubernetes work together to create

---

a secure and scalable secrets management solution. The diagram demonstrates the flow of secrets from Vault to Kubernetes Pods, as well as how Terraform manages the overall infrastructure and configuration.

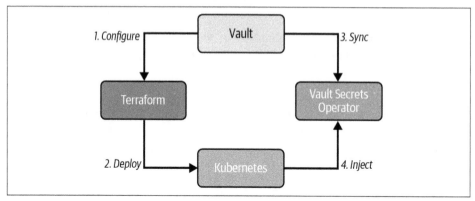

Figure 7-1. Kubernetes Secrets with Vault and Terraform

Solution

To manage Kubernetes Secrets with Vault and Terraform, you can use the Vault provider, the Kubernetes provider, and the Vault Secrets Operator:

```
# Configure the Vault provider
provider "vault" {
  address = "https://vault.example.com"
}

# Configure the Kubernetes provider
provider "kubernetes" {
  config_path = "~/.kube/config"
}

# Enable Kubernetes auth method in Vault
resource "vault_auth_backend" "kubernetes" {
  type = "kubernetes"
}

# Configure Kubernetes auth method
resource "vault_kubernetes_auth_backend_config" "config" {
  backend           = vault_auth_backend.kubernetes.path
  kubernetes_host   = "https://kubernetes.default.svc"
  kubernetes_ca_cert = file("/var/run/secrets/kubernetes.io/serviceaccount/ca.crt")
}

# Create a Vault policy for accessing secrets
resource "vault_policy" "example_policy" {
  name = "example-policy"

  policy = <<EOT
path "secret/data/example/*" {
  capabilities = ["read"]
}
EOT
}
```

```
# Create a Kubernetes service account
resource "kubernetes_service_account" "vault_auth" {
  metadata {
    name = "vault-auth"
  }
}

# Create a Kubernetes secret for the Vault token
resource "kubernetes_secret" "vault_token" {
  metadata {
    name = "vault-token"
  }

  data = {
    token = vault_token.example.client_token
  }
}

# Create a Vault token for Kubernetes auth
resource "vault_token" "example" {
  policies = [vault_policy.example_policy.name]

  renewable = true
  ttl       = "24h"
}

# Install Vault Secrets Operator
resource "helm_release" "vault_secrets_operator" {
  name       = "vault-secrets-operator"
  repository = "https://helm.releases.hashicorp.com"
  chart      = "vault-secrets-operator"
  namespace  = "vault-secrets-operator"

  set {
    name  = "vault.address"
    value = "https://vault.example.com"
  }
}

# Create a VaultStaticSecret resource
resource "kubernetes_manifest" "example_secret" {
  manifest = {
    apiVersion = "secrets.hashicorp.com/v1beta1"
    kind       = "VaultStaticSecret"
    metadata = {
      name = "example-secret"
    }
    spec = {
      vaultAuth = {
        kubernetes = {
          role = "example-role"
          serviceAccount = kubernetes_service_account.vault_auth.metadata[0].name
        }
      }
      mount = "secret"
      type  = "kv-v2"
      path  = "example/mysecret"
      destination = {
        create = true
        name   = "example-k8s-secret"
      }
      refreshAfter = "1h"
    }
```

```
    }
}
```

Discussion

This solution demonstrates how to integrate Vault with Kubernetes using Terraform and the Vault Secrets Operator. Here's a breakdown of the approach:

1. We configure the Vault and Kubernetes providers.
2. We enable and configure the Kubernetes auth method in Vault, which allows Kubernetes to authenticate with Vault.
3. We create a Vault policy that defines the access permissions for our secrets.
4. We create a Kubernetes service account and a Vault token, which will be used for authentication.
5. We install the Vault Secrets Operator using a Helm release. This operator manages the synchronization of secrets between Vault and Kubernetes.
6. Finally, we create a `VaultStaticSecret` resource, which instructs the Vault Secrets Operator to fetch a secret from Vault and create a corresponding Kubernetes Secret.

This approach offers several benefits:

- Centralized secrets management using Vault's advanced features
- Automatic synchronization of secrets between Vault and Kubernetes
- Reduced risk of exposing secrets in Terraform code or version control
- Ability to leverage Vault's dynamic secrets and secret rotation capabilities

When implementing this solution, consider the following best practices:

- Ensure secure communication between Vault, Kubernetes, and Terraform.
- Implement proper access controls and role-based access control (RBAC) in both Vault and Kubernetes.
- Regularly rotate the Vault token used for authentication.
- Monitor and audit access to secrets in both Vault and Kubernetes.

By leveraging Vault's integration with Kubernetes and Terraform, you can establish a robust and secure secrets management workflow for your Kubernetes deployments.

7.5 Storing Secrets as Environment Variables

Problem

When working with secrets in Terraform, one common approach is to store them as environment variables. This method allows you to keep sensitive information out of your Terraform configuration files and provides a convenient way to pass secrets to Terraform during execution.

Solution

This solution demonstrates how to use environment variables to securely pass secrets to Terraform and reference them in your configuration:

```
# Set the secrets as environment variables in your shell or CI/CD pipeline:
# export TF_VAR_database_password="your_database_password"
# export TF_VAR_api_key="your_api_key"

# In your Terraform configuration files, define variables for the secrets:
variable "database_password" {
  description = "Database password"
  type        = string
  sensitive   = true
}

variable "api_key" {
  description = "API key"
  type        = string
  sensitive   = true
}

# Use the variables in your Terraform resource configurations:
resource "example_resource" "example" {
  # ... other configuration ...
  password = var.database_password
  api_key  = var.api_key
}
```

Discussion

In this solution, we start by setting the secrets as environment variables in the shell or CI/CD pipeline where Terraform will be executed. The environment variable names should have the prefix TF_VAR_ followed by the variable name defined in the Terraform configuration. It's important to note that the casing of the environment variable name must match the Terraform variable name exactly.

In the Terraform configuration files, we define variables for the secrets using the variable block. The sensitive attribute is set to true to indicate that the values should be treated as sensitive and not be displayed in plain text in the Terraform output.

Finally, we can use the variables in our Terraform resource configurations by referencing them with the `var` prefix followed by the variable name, such as `var.data base_password` and `var.api_key`.

When Terraform is executed, it automatically picks up the values of the environment variables and assigns them to the corresponding variables defined in the configuration. Storing secrets as environment variables has several benefits:

- Secrets are kept separate from the Terraform configuration files, reducing the risk of accidentally committing sensitive information to version control.
- Environment variables provide a convenient way to pass secrets to Terraform without additional configuration files or external secret management systems.
- It allows for easy integration with CI/CD pipelines, where secrets can be securely stored and passed to Terraform during the execution process.

However, it's essential to consider the following security practices when using environment variables for secrets:

- Ensure that the environment variables are properly secured and not accessible to unauthorized individuals.
- Avoid storing secrets in plain text in scripts or configuration files that set the environment variables.
- Pass secrets to the environment variables using secure methods, such as secret management systems or encrypted files.
- Regularly rotate and update the secrets to maintain their confidentiality.

By following these practices and using environment variables to store secrets, you can effectively manage sensitive information in your Terraform configurations while keeping them secure.

Remember to consider other security measures, such as enabling encryption at rest for the state files and using secure communication channels when interacting with remote backends or APIs.

7.6 Auditing and Rotating Secrets

Problem

When working with secrets in Terraform, it's crucial to have proper auditing and rotation mechanisms in place to ensure the security and integrity of sensitive information. Auditing helps track secret access and usage, while rotation regularly updates secrets to reduce the risk of unauthorized access.

Solution

This solution demonstrates how to implement auditing and rotation of secrets using HashiCorp Vault with Terraform:

```
# Configure the Vault provider
provider "vault" {
  address = "https://vault.example.com"
}

# Retrieve a secret from Vault
data "vault_generic_secret" "example_secret" {
  path = "secret/example"
}

resource "example_resource" "example" {
  # ... other configuration ...
  password = data.vault_generic_secret.example_secret.data["password"]
}

# Enable audit logging in Vault (typically done outside of Terraform)
# vault audit enable file file_path=/var/log/vault_audit.log

# Configure secret rotation policy (example using AWS Secrets Manager)
resource "aws_secretsmanager_secret_rotation" "example" {
  secret_id          = aws_secretsmanager_secret.example.id
  rotation_lambda_arn = aws_lambda_function.rotation_lambda.arn

  rotation_rules {
    automatically_after_days = 30
  }
}
```

Discussion

This solution demonstrates how to integrate Vault with Terraform for secret management, including aspects of auditing and rotation. Here's a breakdown of the approach:

1. We configure the Vault provider to interact with our Vault server.

2. We use the `vault_generic_secret` data source to retrieve secrets from Vault. This ensures that Terraform always uses the latest version of the secret.

3. Auditing is typically enabled on the Vault server itself, not through Terraform. The commented line shows an example of how to enable file-based audit logging in Vault.

4. For secret rotation, we've included an example using AWS Secrets Manager. This resource configures automatic rotation of the secret every 30 days using a Lambda function.

Implementing auditing and rotation offers several benefits:

- Improved security through regular updates of secrets
- Ability to track and review access to secrets

- Compliance with security best practices and regulations

When implementing this solution, consider the following best practices:

- Regularly review audit logs for any suspicious activities.
- Implement proper access controls in Vault and any other secret management systems.
- Ensure that your applications can handle secret rotation gracefully.
- Test the rotation process thoroughly to avoid potential downtime.

By implementing robust auditing and rotation mechanisms, you can significantly enhance the security of your secrets management process in Terraform.

7.7 Managing Secrets with Terraform and Password Managers

Problem

When working with secrets in Terraform, finding a secure and convenient way to manage them is essential. Password managers provide centralized and encrypted storage for secrets, making them a viable option for integration with Terraform.

Solution

This solution demonstrates how to integrate Terraform with a password manager (in this case, 1Password) to retrieve and use secrets securely:

```
# Use the external data source to retrieve secrets from the password manager
data "external" "secrets" {
  program = ["python", "retrieve_secrets.py"]
}

# Use the retrieved secrets in your Terraform resource configurations
resource "example_resource" "example" {
  # ... other configuration ...
  password = data.external.secrets.result.database_password
}

# Content of retrieve_secrets.py:
import json
import subprocess

def retrieve_secrets():
    # Example using 1Password CLI
    password = subprocess.check_output(["op", "get", "item", "database_password"]).decode().strip()
    return {
        "database_password": password
    }

print(json.dumps(retrieve_secrets()))
```

Discussion

This solution demonstrates how to use Terraform's external data source to interact with a password manager. Here's a breakdown of the approach:

1. We use the `external` data source in Terraform to execute a Python script that retrieves secrets from the password manager.
2. The Python script (`retrieve_secrets.py`) uses the 1Password CLI to fetch the required secret. It then returns the secret in a JSON format that Terraform can consume.
3. In the Terraform configuration, we reference the retrieved secret using `data.external.secrets.result.database_password`.

This approach offers several benefits:

- Secrets are stored securely in an encrypted password manager, not in Terraform files.
- Centralized management of secrets across multiple projects and team members.
- Ability to leverage additional features of password managers like access controls and audit logs.

When implementing this solution, consider the following best practices:

- Ensure the script handling secret retrieval is secure and follows best practices for error handling and input validation.
- Use strong authentication for accessing the password manager, preferably with multifactor authentication.
- Regularly rotate secrets stored in the password manager.
- Implement proper access controls in the password manager to limit who can retrieve secrets.

It's important to note that while this method can be effective, it may not be suitable for all environments, especially those with strict security requirements. Always assess the security implications and consider alternatives like dedicated secret management services (e.g., HashiCorp Vault, AWS Secrets Manager) that may offer more robust integration with Terraform.

7.8 Compliance and Governance with Terraform Secrets

Problem

When working with secrets in Terraform, ensuring compliance with security policies and maintaining proper governance over sensitive information is crucial. Compliance requirements may dictate how secrets should be stored, accessed, and audited. Governance involves establishing processes and controls to manage the life cycle of secrets and enforce security best practices.

Solution

This solution outlines a comprehensive approach to achieving compliance and governance for secrets management in Terraform:

```
# Use a compliant secrets management system (e.g., AWS Secrets Manager)
data "aws_secretsmanager_secret_version" "example" {
  secret_id = "example-secret"
}

# Implement access controls
resource "aws_iam_policy" "secret_access_policy" {
  name        = "secret-access-policy"
  description = "Policy for accessing secrets"

  policy = jsonencode({
    Version = "2012-10-17"
    Statement = [
      {
        Effect = "Allow"
        Action = [
          "secretsmanager:GetSecretValue"
        ]
        Resource = data.aws_secretsmanager_secret_version.example.arn
      }
    ]
  })
}

# Use the secret in your resource configuration
resource "example_resource" "example" {
  # ... other configuration ...
  sensitive_data = jsondecode(data.aws_secretsmanager_secret_version.example.secret_string)["key"]
}

# Enable logging and monitoring (example using CloudWatch)
resource "aws_cloudwatch_log_group" "secret_access_logs" {
  name             = "secret-access-logs"
  retention_in_days = 90
}
```

Discussion

This solution demonstrates a multifaceted approach to compliance and governance for secrets management in Terraform:

---

1. We use AWS Secrets Manager as a compliant secrets management system. This ensures secrets are stored securely and can be easily audited.

2. We implement access controls using IAM policies. This restricts access to the secret to only those who need it.

3. The secret is retrieved and used in the Terraform configuration without exposing its value.

4. We set up logging and monitoring using Amazon CloudWatch to track access to secrets.

Key aspects of this approach include:

Secure storage
Using a dedicated secrets management system ensures secrets are encrypted at rest and in transit.

Access control
IAM policies provide fine-grained control over who can access secrets.

Auditing
CloudWatch logs enable tracking of secret access and usage.

Separation of concerns
Secrets are managed separately from Terraform code, reducing the risk of accidental exposure.

When implementing this solution, consider the following best practices:

- Regularly review and update access policies to ensure they adhere to the principle of least privilege.
- Implement secret rotation policies to update secrets periodically.
- Use Terraform workspaces or separate state files to isolate sensitive information for different environments.
- Conduct regular audits of secret usage and access patterns.
- Implement a process for securely onboarding and offboarding team members needing secret access.

By following these practices and implementing a robust compliance and governance framework, you can ensure that your use of Terraform secrets adheres to security best practices and regulatory requirements. This approach helps maintain the confidentiality and integrity of sensitive information throughout your infrastructure management process.

7.9 Dynamic Secrets with HashiCorp Vault

Problem

Static secrets that remain unchanged for long periods can pose security risks if compromised. Dynamic secrets, which are generated on demand and have a limited lifespan, can significantly reduce this risk. HashiCorp Vault provides a solution for generating and managing dynamic secrets.

Solution

This solution demonstrates how to use HashiCorp Vault to generate dynamic database credentials in Terraform:

```
# Configure the Vault provider
provider "vault" {
  address = "https://vault.example.com"
}

# Enable and configure a dynamic secret engine in Vault
resource "vault_mount" "db" {
  path = "database"
  type = "database"
}

resource "vault_database_secret_backend_connection" "mysql" {
  backend       = vault_mount.db.path
  name          = "mysql"
  allowed_roles = ["app"]

  mysql {
    connection_url = "{{username}}:{{password}}@tcp(mysql.example.com:3306)/"
  }
}

resource "vault_database_secret_backend_role" "app" {
  backend     = vault_mount.db.path
  name        = "app"
  db_name     = vault_database_secret_backend_connection.mysql.name
  default_ttl = "1h"
  max_ttl     = "24h"

  creation_statements = [
    "CREATE USER '{{name}}'@'%' IDENTIFIED BY '{{password}}';",
    "GRANT SELECT ON *.* TO '{{name}}'@'%';",
  ]
}

# Generate dynamic credentials
data "vault_database_secret_backend_creds" "creds" {
  backend = vault_mount.db.path
  role    = vault_database_secret_backend_role.app.name
}

# Use the dynamic credentials
resource "mysql_database" "app" {
  name = "app_db"
  user = data.vault_database_secret_backend_creds.creds.username
```

```
    password = data.vault_database_secret_backend_creds.creds.password
}
```

Discussion

This solution sets up and uses dynamic secrets from HashiCorp Vault in Terraform. Here's a breakdown of the approach:

1. We configure the Vault provider to interact with our Vault server.
2. We enable and configure the database secrets engine in Vault, which will generate our dynamic credentials.
3. We set up a database connection and a role that defines how the dynamic credentials will be created.
4. We use the `vault_database_secret_backend_creds` data source to generate dynamic credentials on demand.
5. Finally, we use these dynamic credentials in a resource configuration.

Key benefits of this approach include:

Enhanced security
  Credentials are short-lived and automatically rotated, reducing the risk of compromise.

Simplified management
  Vault handles credential generation and revocation, reducing manual management overhead.

Auditability
  All credential requests can be logged and audited in Vault.

When implementing this solution, consider these best practices:

• Carefully manage the Vault token used by Terraform, ensuring it has only the necessary permissions.
• Set appropriate TTLs for dynamic secrets based on your security requirements and application needs.
• Ensure your applications can handle credential rotation gracefully.
• Regularly audit Vault logs to monitor credential usage and detect any unusual patterns.

By leveraging dynamic secrets with HashiCorp Vault in Terraform, you can significantly enhance the security of your infrastructure management process, reducing the risks associated with long-lived static credentials.

7.10 Securing Secret Injection in CI/CD Pipelines

Problem

When working with CI/CD pipelines, it's common to need access to secrets during the build and deployment process. However, storing these secrets directly in the pipeline configuration or version control system can pose security risks. Secure secret injection is crucial for maintaining the confidentiality of sensitive information in automated workflows (see Figure 7-2).

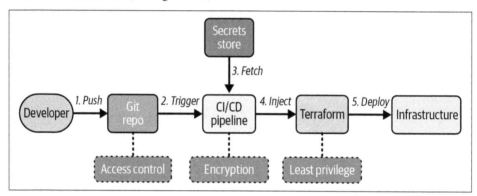

Figure 7-2. Securing secret injection in CI/CD pipelines

Solution

This solution demonstrates how to securely inject secrets into a GitHub Actions workflow when using Terraform:

```yaml
# .github/workflows/terraform.yml
name: Terraform Deployment

on:
  push:
    branches: [main]

jobs:
  deploy:
    runs-on: ubuntu-latest
    steps:
    - uses: actions/checkout@v2

    - name: Configure AWS credentials
      uses: aws-actions/configure-aws-credentials@v1
      with:
        aws-access-key-id: ${{ secrets.AWS_ACCESS_KEY_ID }}
        aws-secret-access-key: ${{ secrets.AWS_SECRET_ACCESS_KEY }}

    - name: Setup Terraform
      uses: hashicorp/setup-terraform@v1

    - name: Terraform Init
      run: terraform init
```

```
    - name: Terraform Apply
      run: terraform apply -auto-approve
      env:
        TF_VAR_database_password: ${{ secrets.DATABASE_PASSWORD }}
        TF_VAR_api_key: ${{ secrets.API_KEY }}


# recipe.tf
variable "database_password" {
  type     = string
  sensitive = true
}

variable "api_key" {
  type     = string
  sensitive = true
}

resource "example_resource" "example" {
  # ... other configuration ...
  password = var.database_password
  api_key  = var.api_key
}
```

Discussion

This solution demonstrates secure secret injection in a GitHub Actions workflow for Terraform deployments. Here's a breakdown of the approach:

1. Secrets are stored securely in GitHub's encrypted secrets storage, not in the workflow file or repository.

2. The workflow uses GitHub's secrets context (`${{ secrets.SECRET_NAME }}`) to access the secrets.

3. Secrets are passed to Terraform as environment variables with the `TF_VAR_` prefix, which Terraform automatically recognizes.

4. In the Terraform configuration, these secrets are defined as sensitive variables and used in resource configurations.

Key benefits of this approach include:

Separation of concerns
    Secrets are managed separately from code and configuration.

Secure storage
    GitHub securely encrypts and manages the secrets.

Limited exposure
    Secrets are only decrypted during runtime and are not logged.

When implementing this solution, consider these best practices:

- Regularly rotate secrets stored in GitHub.
- Use GitHub's RBAC to limit who can access and manage secrets.
- Avoid printing or logging secret values in your Terraform configurations or CI/CD scripts.
- Consider using a dedicated secrets management service (e.g., HashiCorp Vault, AWS Secrets Manager) for more advanced secret management features.

By securely injecting secrets into your CI/CD pipeline, you can automate your Terraform deployments while maintaining the confidentiality of sensitive information. This approach helps prevent unauthorized access to critical credentials and API keys throughout your automated workflows.

## CHAPTER 8

Configuration Management with Terraform

This chapter explores how Terraform can be used for configuration management tasks, ensuring the desired state of system configurations across your infrastructure.

Configuration management involves establishing and maintaining consistency in a system's performance by creating a detailed recording of its information. This information can include details about servers, software, hardware, and other installed components.

Configuration management ensures that all system components operate as intended and that any changes to these components are made systematically to avoid potential disruptions. It's a critical process in modern IT, helping teams automate tasks, boost productivity, and reduce the potential for human errors.

Terraform's primary strength lies in managing infrastructure resources across a broad spectrum of services and providers. While it doesn't directly manage software configurations within servers, it can effectively interact with dedicated configuration management tools, providing a unified and automated method of managing your infrastructure and its configuration.

By the end of this chapter, you'll have a comprehensive understanding of how to use Terraform for various configuration management tasks, enabling you to create more robust and flexible infrastructure-as-code solutions.

8.1 Writing Shell Scripts with Terraform

Problem

You need to automate the creation of infrastructure with Terraform while also running shell scripts on the servers as part of the setup process.

Solution

This solution demonstrates how to use Terraform to create an AWS EC2 instance and execute a shell script on the instance at launch time using the user_data parameter:

```
provider "aws" {
  region = "us-west-2"
}

resource "aws_instance" "example" {
  ami           = "ami-0c94855ba95c574c8"
  instance_type = "t2.micro"

  user_data = <<-EOF
              #!/bin/bash
              echo "Hello, World" > index.html
              nohup busybox httpd -f -p 8080 &
              EOF

  tags = {
    Name = "example-instance"
  }
}
```

Discussion

In this example, we create an AWS EC2 instance in the us-west-2 region using a specific AMI ID and instance type. The key component here is the user_data parameter, which allows us to specify a shell script that will run when the instance launches.

The shell script in this example performs two simple tasks:

- It creates a file named *index.html* with the content "Hello, World".
- It starts a basic HTTP server using busybox on port 8080.

The nohup command is used to run the server in the background, allowing the script to complete and the EC2 instance to start even while the server continues running.

While this is a basic example, the user_data script can be as complex as needed. It can install software, configure settings, start services, and perform any other necessary setup tasks. This makes it a powerful tool for infrastructure automation.

The EOF syntax is used to denote the start and end of the script within the Terraform configuration. For more complex scripts, consider storing them in separate files and loading them using the file() function in Terraform.

The tags block assigns a name to the EC2 instance, making it easier to identify in the AWS console or when using AWS CLI tools.

It's important to note that the user_data script runs only once, when the instance is first launched. If you need to make changes to the instance configuration after it's running, you'll need to use other methods such as SSH access or a configuration management tool like Ansible or Chef.

By combining Terraform's infrastructure provisioning capabilities with shell scripts in user_data, you can create a powerful, automated workflow for setting up and configuring your infrastructure.

8.2 Writing Ansible Configuration with Terraform

Problem

You need to manage your server configuration using Ansible, but you want to bootstrap the servers and provide them with the required Ansible configuration using Terraform.

Solution

This solution demonstrates how to use Terraform to create an AWS EC2 instance, install Ansible, and set up initial Ansible configuration files on the instance at launch time:

```
provider "aws" {
  region = "us-west-2"
}

resource "aws_instance" "example" {
  ami           = "ami-0c94855ba95c574c8"
  instance_type = "t2.micro"

  user_data = <<-EOF
              #!/bin/bash
              apt-get update
              apt-get install -y ansible
              echo "${file("ansible.cfg")}" > /etc/ansible/ansible.cfg
              echo "${file("hosts")}" > /etc/ansible/hosts
              EOF

  tags = {
    Name = "example-instance"
  }
}
```

Discussion

This example builds upon the previous section by demonstrating how to integrate Ansible with Terraform. We create an AWS EC2 instance and use the `user_data` script to set up Ansible on the instance.

The `user_data` script performs the following tasks:

- Updates the package lists using `apt-get update`
- Installs Ansible using `apt-get install -y ansible`
- Copies the contents of a local `ansible.cfg` file to `/etc/ansible/ansible.cfg` on the instance
- Copies the contents of a local `hosts` file to `/etc/ansible/hosts` on the instance

The `file()` function in Terraform is used to read the contents of the local `ansible.cfg` and `hosts` files. This allows you to manage these Ansible configuration files alongside your Terraform code.

Some important considerations:

- This solution assumes you have `ansible.cfg` and `hosts` files in the same directory as your Terraform configuration file. Adjust the paths in the `file()` function if they are located elsewhere.

- The `-y` flag in the `apt-get install -y ansible` command automatically answers `'yes'` to any prompts, allowing the installation to proceed without manual intervention.

- This example uses `apt-get`, which is typical for Ubuntu and Debian-based distributions. If you're using a different Linux distribution, you'll need to adjust the package manager commands accordingly (e.g., use `yum` for Amazon Linux or Red Hat).

- Remember that the `user_data` script only runs once when the instance is first launched. For ongoing configuration management, you would typically use Ansible playbooks after this initial setup.

- In a production environment, you might want to consider more secure ways of distributing your Ansible configuration, such as pulling it from a secure repository or using AWS Systems Manager Parameter Store.

By combining Terraform and Ansible in this way, you can leverage Terraform's strengths in infrastructure provisioning while setting up the groundwork for Ansible to handle more detailed configuration management tasks. This approach provides a powerful, flexible solution for managing both your infrastructure and its configuration.

8.3 Dynamic Configuration with Consul Key-Values

Problem

You need to configure your Terraform-managed infrastructure with dynamic values stored in a Consul key-value store.

Solution

This solution demonstrates how to use Terraform to read configuration values from a Consul key-value store and use those values to configure an AWS EC2 instance:

```
provider "consul" {
  address   = "localhost:8500"
  datacenter = "dc1"
}

data "consul_keys" "app" {
  key {
    name    = "port"
    path    = "app/config/port"
    default = "8080"
  }

  key {
    name    = "name"
    path    = "app/config/name"
    default = "my-app"
  }
}

resource "aws_instance" "example" {
  ami           = "ami-0c94855ba95c574c8"
  instance_type = "t2.micro"

  user_data = <<-EOF
              #!/bin/bash
              echo "App Name: ${data.consul_keys.app.var.name}" > app_config.txt
              echo "App Port: ${data.consul_keys.app.var.port}" >> app_config.txt
              EOF

  tags = {
    Name = "example-instance"
  }
}
```

Discussion

This example showcases how to integrate Consul's key-value store with Terraform for dynamic configuration management. Here's a breakdown of the key components:

1. The consul provider is configured with the address and datacenter of the Consul server. In this example, we're using a public Consul demo server.

2. The `consul_keys` data source is used to read values from the Consul key-value store. We define two keys: `app_port` and `app_name`. For each key, we specify:

name
> A local name used to reference the value in Terraform

path
> The path to the key in the Consul key-value store

default
> A default value to use if the key doesn't exist in Consul

3. In the `aws_instance` resource, we use the values from Consul to create a configuration file on the instance. The `user_data` script writes these values to a file named *app_config.txt*.

4. We access the Consul values using the syntax `${data.consul_keys.app.var.key_name}`. For example, `${data.consul_keys.app.var.name}` retrieves the value for the `name` key.

This approach offers several benefits:

Dynamic configuration
> You can change configuration values in Consul without modifying your Terraform code.

Centralized management
> Consul acts as a central repository for configuration data, which can be used across multiple Terraform projects or other applications.

Default values
> The default attribute provides a fallback if the key doesn't exist in Consul, enhancing reliability.

It's important to note that in a real-world scenario, you would typically use these values to configure your application more comprehensively, not just write them to a file. This example is simplified to demonstrate the principle.

Also, consider security implications when using external data sources like Consul. Ensure that your Consul server is properly secured and that sensitive data is encrypted.

By leveraging Consul with Terraform, you can create more flexible and dynamic infrastructure configurations, allowing for easier management of environment-specific or frequently changing parameters.

8.4 Consuming Data from HTTP Interfaces

Problem

You have an HTTP(S) endpoint that provides configuration data, or any data for that matter, and you want to use this data within your Terraform configuration.

Solution

This solution demonstrates how to use Terraform's HTTP data source to fetch data from an external API and use it within your configuration:

```
data "http" "ip_info" {
  url = "http://ipinfo.io/json"
}

output "ip_info_content_type" {
  value = data.http.ip_info.response_headers["Content-Type"]
}

output "ip_info_body" {
  value = jsondecode(data.http.ip_info.response_body)
}
```

Discussion

This example shows how to use Terraform's HTTP data source to consume data from an external HTTP endpoint. Here's a breakdown of the key components:

1. The HTTP data source is defined with a url attribute specifying the endpoint to query. In this case, we're using the ipinfo.io service, which provides information about the requester's IP address.

2. Terraform makes a GET request to the specified URL when refreshing its state.

3. The response from this request is stored in the http.ip_info data source and can be referenced in other parts of your Terraform configuration.

4. We define two outputs to demonstrate how to access the data:

    a. ip_info_content_type accesses the Content-Type header from the response.

    b. ip_info_body accesses the body of the response. We use the jsondecode function to parse the JSON response into a Terraform object.

Key points to consider when using the HTTP data source:

- By default, the HTTP data source sends a GET request. If you need to use a different method or include headers, you can use the request_headers and method attributes.

- The body of the response is stored as a string. If the HTTP endpoint returns JSON (as in this example), you should use the `jsondecode` function to parse it into a Terraform object for easier manipulation.

- Be cautious when using external data sources in your Terraform configurations. Ensure that the endpoints you're querying are reliable and that you're handling potential errors or unexpected data appropriately.

- Consider caching mechanisms or using local variables if you need to reference the data multiple times in your configuration to avoid unnecessary API calls.

- For sensitive data, always use HTTPS endpoints and consider using Terraform's sensitive output feature to prevent the data from being displayed in logs or console output.

This approach allows you to incorporate dynamic, external data into your Terraform configurations, enabling more flexible and responsive infrastructure management. You could use this technique to fetch configuration data, incorporate real-time information into your resources, or dynamically adjust your infrastructure based on external factors.

8.5 Applying Conditional Logic in Terraform

Problem

You need to create resources in Terraform only under certain conditions, such as creating an AWS EC2 instance only when a specific variable is set to true.

Solution

This solution demonstrates how to use conditional logic in Terraform to create resources based on a boolean variable:

```
variable "create_instance" {
  description = "Control whether an EC2 instance should be created"
  type        = bool
  default     = false
}

resource "aws_instance" "example" {
  count         = var.create_instance ? 1 : 0
  ami           = "ami-0c94855ba95c574c8"
  instance_type = "t2.micro"

  tags = {
    Name = "example-instance"
  }
}
```

Discussion

This example illustrates how to use conditional logic in Terraform to control resource creation. Here's a breakdown of the key components:

1. We define a variable `create_instance` of type `bool` with a default value of `false`. This variable will control whether the EC2 instance is created.

2. In the `aws_instance` resource block, we use the count parameter to conditionally create the instance. The count parameter uses a ternary operator:

   a. If `create_instance` is `true`, count will be 1, and one instance will be created.

   b. If `create_instance` is `false`, count will be 0, and no instance will be created.

3. The rest of the `aws_instance` resource block defines the instance configuration as usual.

Key points to consider when using conditional logic in Terraform:

1. The `count` parameter is a powerful tool for conditional resource creation. When count is 0, Terraform doesn't create the resource at all.

2. You can use more complex expressions in the `ternary` operator if needed, but it's often clearer to compute complex conditions in a local value and reference that in the `count` parameter.

3. Be cautious when using conditional logic with existing resources. If you change the condition to `false` for an existing resource, Terraform will destroy that resource on the next apply.

4. Remember that when using `count`, Terraform treats the resource as a list. If you need to reference a conditionally created resource elsewhere in your configuration, you'll need to use the index syntax (e.g., `aws_instance.example[0]`).

5. For more complex conditions, you might want to consider using the `for_each` meta-argument instead of `count`. `for_each` can provide more flexibility and make it easier to add or remove individual resources without affecting others.

6. This pattern can be applied to any resource in Terraform, not just EC2 instances. It's a versatile technique for creating flexible, dynamic infrastructure configurations.

It's important to note that while conditional logic in Terraform is powerful, it can also lead to potential issues:

- Toggling the `create_instance` variable frequently could lead to unintended resource destruction and recreation. This might cause data loss or downtime if not managed carefully.

- In more complex scenarios, the interdependencies between conditionally created resources can become difficult to manage and reason about.

- Overuse of conditional logic can make your Terraform configurations harder to understand and maintain.

To mitigate these risks, consider using Terraform workspaces or separate configuration files for significantly different environments or configurations. Reserve conditional logic for cases where the differences are minor and well-understood.

By leveraging conditional logic judiciously, you can create more dynamic and flexible Terraform configurations that adapt to different environments or requirements without sacrificing clarity or maintainability.

8.6 Importing Existing Infrastructure into Terraform

Problem

You have existing infrastructure that was created outside of Terraform (manually or using a different tool), and you need to bring it under Terraform management.

Solution

This solution demonstrates how to import existing infrastructure into Terraform using the `terraform import` command and the new config-driven import feature.

First, define a resource block in your Terraform configuration corresponding to the existing infrastructure:

```
resource "aws_instance" "imported" {
  # The instance ID will be filled in after import
  ami          = "ami-0c94855ba95c574c8"
  instance_type = "t2.micro"
  tags = {
    Name = "ImportedInstance"
  }
}

import {
  to = aws_instance.imported
  id = "i-1234567890abcdef0"
}
```

Then, to import the existing infrastructure into Terraform, use the `terraform import` command:

```
terraform init
terraform plan -generate-config-out=generated_resources.tf
```

Discussion

Importing existing resources into Terraform allows you to bring previously created resources under Terraform management. This is particularly useful when transitioning from manual management or another IaC tool to Terraform.

Key points to consider:

Config-driven import

The example uses the newer config-driven import feature, which is preferred over the CLI-based import commands. This approach allows you to define the import configuration directly in your Terraform files, making it easier to version control and manage imports.

Resource definition

Before importing, you need to define the resource in your configuration. The configuration doesn't need to be complete initially; you just need to ensure the resource block exists.

Import block

The import block specifies which resource to import (`to`) and the resource's ID in the provider (`id`). For an EC2 instance, this would be the instance ID.

Generate config

The `terraform plan -generate-config-out=generated_resources.tf` command will generate a new file with the complete resource configuration based on the actual state of the imported resource.

State management

After import, Terraform will manage the resource's state, but it won't automatically generate or update your configuration to match the imported resource's current settings. You'll need to manually update your configuration to match the imported resource's current state.

Provider-specific

The ability to import a resource and the ID format required depends on the specific Terraform provider. Always refer to the provider's documentation for the correct import syntax and requirements.

Partial import

Not all attributes of a resource may be importable. Some may need to be set manually in your configuration after import.

Caution with sensitive data

Be careful when importing resources that might contain sensitive data. Ensure that such data is properly managed and secured in your Terraform configuration.

By using the config-driven import feature, you can more easily manage and version control your import process, making it a more integral part of your IaC workflow. This approach is especially beneficial when working in teams or managing complex infrastructures where tracking imports is crucial.

8.7 Leveraging Terraform Workspaces

Problem

You need to manage multiple environments (e.g., development, staging, and production) for your infrastructure. You want to use the same Terraform configuration for all environments but need to ensure isolation between them.

Solution

This solution demonstrates managing multiple environments using Terraform workspaces, ensuring isolation and consistency across different environments. The same Terraform configuration can be used while maintaining separate state files for each environment.

First, create a new workspace using the `terraform workspace new` command:

```
terraform workspace new dev
```

Next, modify your Terraform configuration to use the workspace key to differentiate resources by environment:

```
provider "aws" {
  region = "us-west-2"
}

resource "aws_instance" "example" {
  ami           = "ami-0c94855ba95c574c8"
  instance_type = "t2.micro"

  tags = {
    Name        = "example-instance-${terraform.workspace}"
    Environment = terraform.workspace
  }
}
```

Discussion

Terraform workspaces allow you to manage multiple environments such as development, staging, and production, with the same configuration but in an isolated manner. Each workspace maintains its own separate state file, which means resources created in one workspace do not interfere with resources in another.

Key points to consider:

Creating a workspace

The `terraform workspace new dev` command creates a new workspace named dev. Terraform will automatically switch to this workspace upon creation.

Using workspace in configuration

In your Terraform configuration, the `terraform.workspace` interpolation is used to get the name of the current workspace. This can be utilized to set tags or differentiate resources based on the workspace. In the example configuration, `terraform.workspace` is used to set the `Name` and `Environment` tags for the AWS instance, helping in differentiating resources between environments:

Switching workspaces

You can switch between workspaces using the `terraform workspace select <workspace_name>` command. Applying the configuration with `terraform apply` will then apply changes to the selected workspace.

Isolated state files

Each workspace has its own state file, ensuring that resources in one workspace do not affect those in another. This isolation is crucial for managing different environments efficiently.

Consistency across environments

By using workspaces, you can ensure that the same Terraform configuration is applied consistently across different environments, reducing the risk of configuration drift.

Workspace-specific resource management

The use of the `terraform.workspace` interpolation ensures that resources are tagged and managed appropriately for each environment, making it easier to track and manage resources in the AWS console or CLI.

Best practices

Ensure your configuration is designed to handle workspace-specific settings and state data, especially when referencing data across workspaces.

By leveraging workspaces, you can streamline the management of multiple environments using a single Terraform configuration, ensuring consistency and isolation. This approach simplifies the process of maintaining different environments and helps in managing infrastructure more efficiently.

8.8 Utilizing Terraform Templates

Problem

You need to configure a resource with a multiline or complex configuration. For instance, you have a `cloud-init userdata` script for an EC2 instance, and you want to manage this script as part of your Terraform configuration.

Solution

This solution demonstrates how to manage complex configurations using Terraform templates, ensuring maintainability and separation of concerns.

First, create a template file, for example, *user_data.tpl*:

```
#cloud-config
hostname: ${hostname}
fqdn: ${hostname}.example.com
manage_etc_hosts: true
```

Next, utilize the template within your configuration:

```
provider "aws" {
  region = "us-west-2"
}

data "template_file" "user_data" {
  template = file("${path.module}/user_data.tpl")

  vars = {
    hostname = "webserver"
  }
}

resource "aws_instance" "example" {
  ami           = "ami-0c94855ba95c574c8"
  instance_type = "t2.micro"

  user_data = data.template_file.user_data.rendered
}
```

Discussion

Using Terraform templates allows for a clean separation between your Terraform configuration and complex multiline scripts or configurations. This approach is beneficial for maintainability, readability, and version control.

Key points to consider:

Template file
> The *user_data.tpl* file contains the cloud-init configuration. This file can be as complex as needed, and separating it from the Terraform configuration makes it easier to manage.

Template data source

The `template_file` data source is used to read and render the template file. The `template` argument reads the file from the filesystem, while the `vars` argument passes variables into the template.

Variable interpolation

In the template file, `${hostname}` is a placeholder for the variable. This is replaced by the value specified in the `vars` block in the Terraform configuration.

Resource configuration

The `aws_instance` resource uses the rendered template for the `user_data` argument. The `data.template_file.user_data.rendered` reference ensures the correct configuration is applied to the EC2 instance.

Maintainability

Separating scripts and configurations into template files allows for easier updates and maintenance. It also enables you to reuse templates across different Terraform configurations.

Version control

Template files can be checked into version control systems such as Git, providing a history of changes and facilitating collaboration.

Extensibility

Terraform's template language is based on Go templates, which allows for powerful features such as conditionals and loops. This enables the creation of dynamic and flexible configurations.

By utilizing Terraform templates, you can manage complex configurations more effectively, ensuring that your infrastructure as code remains clean, maintainable, and scalable. This approach is particularly useful when dealing with intricate setups or when you need to apply consistent configurations across multiple resources.

8.9 Managing Dependencies Between Terraform Resources

Problem

You have multiple Terraform resources and need to ensure they are created or destroyed in a specific order due to dependencies between them.

Solution

This solution demonstrates how to manage dependencies between Terraform resources using implicit and explicit dependency mechanisms:

```
provider "aws" {
  region = "us-west-2"
}

resource "aws_security_group" "sg" {
  name = "example-sg"
}

resource "aws_instance" "example" {
  ami           = "ami-0c94855ba95c574c8"
  instance_type = "t2.micro"

  vpc_security_group_ids = [aws_security_group.sg.id]

  depends_on = [
    aws_security_group.sg
  ]
}
```

Discussion

Terraform automatically manages dependencies between resources based on attribute references, ensuring resources are created or destroyed in the correct order. However, there are scenarios where explicit dependencies must be defined:

Implicit dependencies

Dependencies are usually inferred from resource attribute references. In the example, the `aws_instance` resource references the `aws_security_group` resource through the `vpc_security_group_ids` attribute. This creates an implicit dependency, ensuring the security group is created before the instance.

Explicit dependencies

In cases where implicit dependencies are not sufficient, the `depends_on` argument can be used to specify explicit dependencies. In the example, the `depends_on` argument ensures the `aws_instance` resource is created only after the `aws_security_group` resource, even if there were no direct attribute references.

Best practices

Rely on implicit dependencies

Whenever possible, use attribute references to create implicit dependencies. This keeps your configuration clean and easy to maintain.

Use `depends_on` sparingly

Resort to explicit dependencies only when necessary to enforce a specific order that Terraform cannot infer automatically.

Resource creation order

Be mindful of the order in which resources are created, especially when dealing with critical dependencies that could impact your infrastructure's stability.

Performance considerations

Using implicit dependencies allows Terraform to create resources in parallel when there are no dependencies, speeding up the execution of your configuration. Explicit dependencies can limit parallelism and slow down the process.

By managing dependencies effectively, you ensure that your Terraform configurations are robust and reliable. Proper dependency management prevents issues arising from resources being created or destroyed in an incorrect order, ensuring smooth infrastructure provisioning and maintenance.

8.10 Using Terraform for Blue-Green Deployments

Problem

You want to ensure zero downtime when deploying your application. You want to implement a blue-green deployment strategy using Terraform to achieve this. Figure 8-1 illustrates this concept, showing how traffic can be switched between the two environments during a deployment. This approach allows you to test the new version of your application in the green environment before switching the traffic, ensuring a smooth transition with minimal risk.

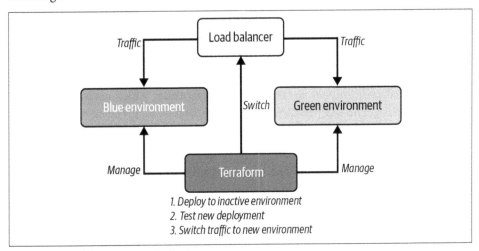

Figure 8-1. A blue-green style deployment

Solution

This solution demonstrates how to perform blue-green deployments using AWS Elastic Load Balancing (ELB) and two sets of EC2 instances (blue and green).

First, define a variable to control the deployment environment:

```
variable "color" {
  description = "Deployed environment color: blue or green"
  default     = "blue"
}

provider "aws" {
  region = "us-west-2"
}

resource "aws_instance" "blue" {
  count         = var.color == "blue" ? 2 : 0
  ami           = "ami-0c94855ba95c574c8"
  instance_type = "t2.micro"
}

resource "aws_instance" "green" {
  count         = var.color == "green" ? 2 : 0
  ami           = "ami-0c94855ba95c574c8"
  instance_type = "t2.micro"
}

resource "aws_elb" "example" {
  instances = concat(aws_instance.blue.*.id, aws_instance.green.*.id)

  # other configurations...
}
```

Discussion

Blue-green deployments involve running two identical production environments, one live (blue) and one idle (green). This strategy ensures zero downtime by switching the live environment to the new version once it is fully tested.

In the provided code snippet, a variable color determines which environment (blue or green) is active. The aws_instance resources for blue and green environments are conditionally created based on this variable. Only one set of instances (either blue or green) is created at a time, depending on the value of color.

The aws_elb resource is configured to route traffic to both sets of instances. The concat function is used to combine the instance IDs of both blue and green environments. This setup ensures that the load balancer can direct traffic to either environment.

When switching environments, you change the value of the color variable and apply the configuration with terraform apply. This process creates a new set of instances, adds them to the load balancer, and then destroys the old instances, achieving a seamless switch.

While the provided example is simplified, real-world blue-green deployments can be more complex. They may involve database migrations, stateful components, and additional infrastructure considerations. Extensive testing in the idle environment is crucial before making it live to ensure the new version works correctly.

Using Terraform for blue-green deployments helps manage infrastructure changes efficiently and reliably, reducing the risk of downtime and ensuring a smooth transition between application versions.

## CHAPTER 9

Advanced Terraform Techniques

This chapter delves into advanced Terraform techniques that will elevate your infrastructure management skills. We'll explore complex scenarios and sophisticated functionalities designed to help you tackle the multifaceted challenges of modern infrastructure management.

Our focus is enhancing your Terraform proficiency beyond the basics, guiding you through intricate concepts and strategies for managing large-scale, dynamic, and multicloud environments. You'll gain insights into optimizing Terraform for scalable architectures, developing custom providers for unique use cases, and seamlessly integrating Terraform with various monitoring and compliance tools. We'll also address the intricacies of debugging complex Terraform projects, presenting methods to dissect and resolve challenging issues effectively.

By the end of this chapter, you'll have a comprehensive understanding of advanced Terraform techniques. This knowledge will empower you to architect robust, efficient infrastructure solutions, ensuring your Terraform skills are at the forefront of industry standards and practices. Whether managing expansive cloud ecosystems or orchestrating multitiered applications, the expertise gained here will be pivotal in your journey as an advanced Terraform practitioner.

Each section provides practical examples and in-depth discussions to help you master these advanced concepts and apply them effectively in your infrastructure management workflows.

9.1 Writing Configuration Files with Terraform

Problem

As infrastructure complexity grows, managing Terraform configurations becomes increasingly challenging. Monolithic configurations are difficult to maintain, reuse, and scale.

Solution

This solution demonstrates how to create modular Terraform configurations for improved organization, reusability, and maintainability:

```
# main.tf
module "network" {
  source     = "./modules/network"
  vpc_cidr   = "10.0.0.0/16"
  subnet_cidrs = ["10.0.1.0/24", "10.0.2.0/24"]
}

module "compute" {
  source     = "./modules/compute"
  subnet_id = module.network.subnet_ids[0]
  instance_type = "t3.micro"
}

# modules/network/main.tf
resource "aws_vpc" "main" {
  cidr_block = var.vpc_cidr
}

resource "aws_subnet" "main" {
  count      = length(var.subnet_cidrs)
  vpc_id     = aws_vpc.main.id
  cidr_block = var.subnet_cidrs[count.index]
}

output "subnet_ids" {
  value = aws_subnet.main[*].id
}

# modules/compute/main.tf
resource "aws_instance" "main" {
  subnet_id     = var.subnet_id
  instance_type = var.instance_type
  ami           = "ami-0c55b159cbfafe1f0"  # Amazon Linux 2 AMI
}
```

To implement this modular approach:

1. Create separate directories for each module (for example, modules/network, or modules/compute).

2. Define input variables and outputs for each module.

3. In the root module, call the child modules and pass the necessary variables.

Discussion

Modular Terraform configurations offer several benefits:

Reusability
Modules can be reused across different projects or environments, promoting consistent infrastructure patterns.

Maintainability
Smaller, focused modules are easier to understand and maintain than large, monolithic configurations.

Abstraction
Modules hide complex implementation details, allowing users to focus on high-level configuration.

Testing
Modules can be tested independently, improving overall code quality.

Version control
Modules can be versioned, enabling better change management and rollback capabilities.

When designing modules:

- Keep modules focused on a specific function or resource group.
- Use clear, descriptive names for modules, variables, and outputs.
- Document module usage, including required and optional variables.
- Consider using a consistent structure across modules for easier navigation.

By adopting a modular approach, you can significantly improve the scalability and manageability of your Terraform configurations, especially in large or complex infrastructure setups.

9.2 Writing Cloud-Init Configuration

Problem

Managing multiple environments (e.g., development, staging, production) with Terraform can lead to code duplication and increased complexity when using separate configuration files for each environment.

Solution

This solution demonstrates how to use Terraform workspaces to manage multiple environments using a single set of configuration files:

```
# main.tf
provider "aws" {
  region = "us-west-2"
}

locals {
  environment_config = {
    default = {
      instance_type = "t3.micro"
      instance_count = 1
    }
    staging = {
      instance_type = "t3.small"
      instance_count = 2
    }
    production = {
      instance_type = "t3.medium"
      instance_count = 3
    }
  }

  config = lookup(
    local.environment_config,
    terraform.workspace,
    local.environment_config["default"])
}

resource "aws_instance" "app_server" {
  count         = local.config.instance_count
  ami           = "ami-0c55b159cbfafe1f0"
  instance_type = local.config.instance_type

  tags = {
    Name = "AppServer-${terraform.workspace}-${count.index + 1}"
    Environment = terraform.workspace
  }
}
```

To use Terraform workspaces:

1. Initialize your Terraform configuration: `terraform init`.

2. Create workspaces for each environment:

   ```
   terraform workspace new development
   terraform workspace new staging
   terraform workspace new production
   ```

3. Switch to the desired workspace before applying: `terraform workspace select staging`.

4. Apply the configuration: `terraform apply`.

Discussion

Terraform workspaces provide a powerful way to manage multiple environments using a single set of configuration files. This approach offers several advantages:

Code reuse
You maintain a single set of configuration files for all environments, reducing duplication and potential inconsistencies.

Environment isolation
Each workspace has its own state file, ensuring that operations in one environment don't affect others.

Flexible configuration
Use the `terraform.workspace` variable to apply environment-specific settings, as demonstrated in the example.

Simplified workflow
Easily switch between environments using workspace commands, streamlining the deployment process.

When using workspaces, consider the following best practices:

- Use consistent naming conventions for workspaces across projects.
- Implement strict access controls, especially for production workspaces.
- Use remote state storage with workspaces to enable team collaboration.
- Consider using workspaces in combination with variables files for more complex configurations.

While workspaces are powerful, they may not be suitable for all scenarios. For highly disparate environments or when working with multiple regions or accounts, separate configuration files might be more appropriate.

You can efficiently manage multiple environments by leveraging Terraform workspaces, reducing complexity and ensuring consistency across your infrastructure deployments.

9.3 Implementing Terraform Modules in CI/CD Pipelines

Problem

Manually applying Terraform changes can be error-prone and time-consuming, especially in large-scale, collaborative environments. There's a need to automate and standardize the infrastructure deployment process.

Solution

This solution demonstrates how to integrate Terraform into a CI/CD pipeline using GitHub Actions, enabling automated testing, planning, and applying of infrastructure changes:

```
# .github/workflows/terraform.yml
name: 'Terraform CI/CD'

on:
  push:
    branches: [ "main" ]
  pull_request:
    branches: [ "main" ]

jobs:
  terraform:
    name: 'Terraform'
    runs-on: ubuntu-latest

    steps:
    - name: Checkout
      uses: actions/checkout@v3

    - name: Setup Terraform
      uses: hashicorp/setup-terraform@v2

    - name: Terraform Init
      run: terraform init

    - name: Terraform Format
      run: terraform fmt -check

    - name: Terraform Validate
      run: terraform validate

    - name: Terraform Plan
      run: terraform plan -no-color
      if: github.event_name == 'pull_request'

    - name: Terraform Apply
      if: github.ref == 'refs/heads/main' && github.event_name == 'push'
      run: terraform apply -auto-approve
```

To implement this CI/CD pipeline:

1. Create the *.github/workflows/terraform.yml* file in your repository.
2. Configure your cloud provider credentials as GitHub secrets.
3. Adjust the workflow as needed for your specific setup (e.g., adding environment-specific steps).

Discussion

Integrating Terraform with CI/CD pipelines offers several benefits:

Automation
Reduces manual errors and speeds up the deployment process

Consistency
Ensures that infrastructure changes go through a standardized process

Validation
Automatically checks for formatting issues and validates configurations before applying

Collaboration
Facilitates code reviews for infrastructure changes through pull requests

Auditability
Provides a clear history of infrastructure changes tied to code commits

When implementing Terraform in CI/CD pipelines, consider the following best practices:

- Use remote state storage (e.g., S3, Azure Blob Storage) to enable collaboration and maintain state consistency.
- Implement state locking to prevent concurrent modifications.
- Use workspaces or separate state files for different environments (dev, staging, prod).
- Secure sensitive information using environment variables or secure secret management solutions.
- Implement approval processes for applying changes to production environments.
- Consider using HCP Terraform or Terraform Enterprise for enhanced collaboration and governance features.

Advanced considerations:

- Implement custom validation steps or policy checks (e.g., using OPI) in your pipeline.
- Use dynamic environments for feature branches to test infrastructure changes.
- Implement drift detection to identify manual changes outside of Terraform.
- Consider using Terragrunt for managing multienvironment deployments and keeping your Terraform configurations DRY (Don't Repeat Yourself).

By integrating Terraform with CI/CD pipelines, you can achieve a more robust, reliable, and efficient infrastructure deployment process, enabling teams to manage complex infrastructures at scale with confidence.

9.4 Advanced State Management in Terraform

Problem

Managing Terraform state becomes increasingly complex in large-scale, multiteam environments. Issues such as state locking conflicts, managing sensitive data, and handling state refactoring can hinder productivity and pose security risks.

Solution

This solution demonstrates advanced state management techniques including state locking, secure handling of sensitive data, and state manipulation:

```
# backend.tf
terraform {
  backend "s3" {
    bucket         = "my-terraform-state-bucket"
    key            = "path/to/my/key"
    region         = "us-west-2"
    encrypt        = true
    kms_key_id     = "arn:aws:kms:us-west-2:111122223333:key/1234abcd-12ab-34cd-56ef-1234567890ab"
    dynamodb_table = "terraform-locks"
  }
}

# main.tf
resource "aws_db_instance" "example" {
  # ... other configuration ...
  password = var.db_password
}

# variables.tf
variable "db_password" {
  type        = string
  sensitive   = true
  description = "Password for the database"
}
```

To implement these techniques:

1. Configure a remote backend with encryption and state locking.

2. Use sensitive variables for managing secrets.

3. Utilize state manipulation commands for refactoring:

   a. `terraform state mv` for moving resources

   b. `terraform state rm` for removing resources from state

   c. `terraform import` for importing existing resources

Discussion

Advanced state management is crucial for maintaining security, consistency, and efficiency in complex Terraform deployments:

- State locking:
  - This prevents concurrent state modifications, reducing the risk of conflicts.
  - Implement this by using DynamoDB for AWS or Azure Storage for Azure.
- Encryption:
  - Encryption protects sensitive data in the state file.
  - Use server-side encryption with KMS for added security.
- Sensitive data handling:
  - Mark variables as sensitive to prevent their values from appearing in logs.
  - Consider using external secret management systems (e.g., HashiCorp Vault) for highly sensitive data.
- State manipulation:
  - `terraform state mv` is useful for refactoring, moving resources between modules without destroying and re-creating them.
  - `terraform state rm` helps manage resources that should no longer be managed by Terraform.
  - `terraform import` allows bringing existing resources under Terraform management.
- State backup and versioning:
  - Enable versioning on your state storage (e.g., S3 bucket versioning) to maintain a history of state changes.
  - Implement regular backups of your state files.
- Partial configuration:
  - Use partial backend configuration to separate sensitive backend details from version-controlled code.
- State migration:
  - When changing backend types, use `terraform init -migrate-state` to safely migrate your state.
- Workspaces for environment separation:

— Utilize Terraform workspaces to manage multiple environments (dev, staging, prod) with separate states.

Advanced considerations:

- Implement state file monitoring for detecting unauthorized changes.
- Use state file encryption-at-rest and in-transit for maximum security.
- Consider using HCP Terraform or Terraform Enterprise for advanced state management features, including state locking, versioning, and access controls.
- For very large infrastructures, consider splitting state into multiple smaller states to improve performance and reduce the blast radius of potential issues.

By implementing these advanced state management techniques, you can enhance the security, reliability, and maintainability of your Terraform-managed infrastructure, especially in complex, multiteam environments.

9.5 Terraform and Multicloud Strategies

Problem

Managing large-scale, dynamic infrastructures with Terraform can become complex and unwieldy, especially when dealing with numerous similar resources or when resource creation needs to be conditional or data driven.

Solution

This solution demonstrates advanced resource management techniques in Terraform, including dynamic resource creation using for_each and for expressions and local values for complex data transformations.

Here is an example of a multicloud Terraform configuration managing resources in both AWS and Azure:

```
locals {
  environments = ["dev", "stg", "prd"]
  instance_types = {
    dev     = "t3.micro"
    staging = "t3.small"
    prod    = "t3.medium"
  }

  instances = {
    for env in local.environments : env => {
      type  = local.instance_types[env]
      count = env == "prd" ? 3 : 1
    }
  }
}
```

```
resource "aws_instance" "app_servers" {
  for_each = local.instances

  ami           = "ami-0c55b159cbfafe1f0"
  instance_type = each.value.type
  count         = each.value.count

  tags = {
    Name = "AppServer-${each.key}-${count.index + 1}"
    Environment = each.key
  }
}

output "instance_ips" {
  value = {
    for env, instances in aws_instance.app_servers : env => [
      for instance in instances : instance.private_ip
    ]
  }
}
```

This configuration:

- Defines environments and instance types using local values
- Uses a for expression to create a map of instance configurations
- Employs for_each to create instances for each environment
- Utilizes count within for_each for varying numbers of instances per environment
- Generates a structured output of instance IPs using nested for expressions

Discussion

This approach addresses several advanced Terraform techniques and best practices:

Dynamic resource creation
Using for_each with a map allows for dynamic creation of resources based on complex criteria. This is more efficient and easier to manage than using count for conditional resource creation, as suggested by the reviewers.

Local values for data transformation
Local values are used to transform and prepare data, keeping the resource blocks clean and focused on resource definition. This separation of data preparation and resource creation improves readability and maintainability.

Conditional resource attributes
The solution demonstrates how to conditionally set resource attributes (like instance count) based on the environment.

Complex outputs

The output block shows how to generate structured data from resources created with for_each and count, providing a clear view of the created infrastructure.

Scalability

This approach scales well for managing many similar resources across different environments or configurations.

Readability and maintainability

By using descriptive names for locals and resources, the configuration remains readable even as it grows in complexity.

When implementing these techniques, consider:

State management

With dynamic resource creation, be cautious when making changes that could affect resource addresses, as this could cause unexpected resource re-creation.

Module design

These techniques can be particularly powerful when used in reusable modules.

Performance

While for_each and for expressions are powerful, overuse in very large configurations could impact the Terraform life cycle times.

Debugging

Complex expressions can make debugging more challenging. Use terraform console to test and verify your expressions.

By leveraging these advanced resource management techniques, you can create more flexible, maintainable, and scalable Terraform configurations, addressing the complexities of managing large-scale, dynamic infrastructure as highlighted by the tech reviewers.

9.6 Terraform for Scalable Architectures

Problem

Managing large-scale Terraform projects across multiple environments and teams poses challenges in terms of code organization, reusability, and maintainability. Traditional approaches can lead to code duplication and difficulty in managing complex infrastructure relationships.

Solution

This solution demonstrates advanced techniques for managing large-scale Terraform projects, including using multiple root modules, dynamic module generation, and managing common modules across teams:

```
# project_structure.tf
locals {
  environments = ["dev", "stg", "prd"]
  regions      = ["us-west-2", "eu-west-1"]

  deployments = {
    for pair in setproduct(local.environments, local.regions) :
    "${pair[0]}-${pair[1]}" => {
      env    = pair[0]
      region = pair[1]
    }
  }
}

module "deployments" {
  source   = "./modules/deployment"
  for_each = local.deployments

  environment = each.value.env
  region      = each.value.region
  vpc_cidr    = var.vpc_cidrs[each.key]
}

# modules/deployment/main.tf
module "network" {
  source   = "git::https://github.com/org/tf-modules.git//network?ref=v1.2.0"
  env      = var.environment
  region   = var.region
  vpc_cidr = var.vpc_cidr
}

module "compute" {
  source     = "git::https://github.com/org/tf-modules.git//compute?ref=v1.2.0"
  env        = var.environment
  subnet_ids = module.network.subnet_ids
}

# variables.tf
variable "vpc_cidrs" {
  type = map(string)
}

# terraform.tfvars
vpc_cidrs = {
  "dev-us-west-2"     = "10.0.0.0/16"
  "dev-eu-west-1"     = "10.1.0.0/16"
  "staging-us-west-2" = "10.2.0.0/16"
  "staging-eu-west-1" = "10.3.0.0/16"
  "prod-us-west-2"    = "10.4.0.0/16"
  "prod-eu-west-1"    = "10.5.0.0/16"
}
```

This configuration demonstrates:

- Dynamic generation of deployments across multiple environments and regions

- Use of a common deployment module to ensure consistency
- Referencing shared modules from a centralized repository

Discussion

This approach addresses several advanced techniques for managing large-scale Terraform projects:

Multiple root modules
> Instead of using a single monolithic configuration, this approach uses a root module that dynamically generates deployments. This allows for easier management of multiple environments and regions.

Dynamic module generation
> The `setproduct` function and `for` expression are used to dynamically generate a map of deployments. This approach is highly scalable and reduces code duplication.

Common module management
> Shared modules are referenced from a centralized Git repository with version pinning. This ensures consistency across teams and allows for versioned updates.

Environment-specific configurations
> The use of variables (such as `vpc_cidrs`) allows for environment-specific configurations without changing the core module structure.

Code reusability
> The deployment module encapsulates the core infrastructure components, promoting reuse across different environments and regions.

Additional considerations for large-scale projects:

State management
> For very large projects, consider using separate state files for different components or environments. Tools such as Terragrunt can help manage this complexity.

CI/CD integration
> Implement a robust CI/CD pipeline that can handle testing and deploying changes across multiple environments.

Policy as code
> Implement policy-as-code solutions (e.g., OPA, Sentinel) to enforce standards across all deployments.

Module development workflow
> Establish a clear process for developing, testing, and releasing shared modules.

Documentation
   Maintain comprehensive documentation for shared modules and overall architecture.

Terraform version management
   Use tools such as `tfenv` to manage Terraform versions across different projects and teams.

Performance optimization
   For very large projects, consider techniques such as `-target` for focused applies, and optimize module structures to reduce plan/apply times.

By implementing these advanced techniques, you can effectively manage large-scale Terraform projects, addressing the complexities of multienvironment, multiregion deployments while maintaining code quality and consistency across teams.

9.7 Terraform Custom Provider Development

Problem

Complex infrastructure requirements often demand more dynamic and flexible Terraform configurations. Static configurations can lead to code duplication and difficulty in adapting to changing requirements.

Solution

This solution demonstrates the advanced use of Terraform functions and expressions to create highly dynamic and flexible configurations:

```
locals {
  environments = ["dev", "stg", "prd"]
  regions = {
    us = ["us-east-1", "us-west-2"]
    eu = ["eu-west-1", "eu-central-1"]
  }

  # Generate all combinations of environment and region
  deployments = flatten([
    for env in local.environments : [
      for continent, areas in local.regions : [
        for region in areas : {
          env       = env
          continent = continent
          region    = region
        }
      ]
    ]
  ])

  # Define instance types based on environment and continent
  instance_types = {
    dev   = { us = "t3.micro",  eu = "t3.small" }
    stg = { us = "t3.small",  eu = "t3.medium" }
```

```
    prd     = { us = "t3.medium", eu = "t3.large" }
  }

  # Generate VPC CIDRs dynamically
  vpc_cidrs = {
    for idx, deployment in local.deployments :
    "${deployment.env}-${deployment.region}" => cidrsubnet("10.0.0.0/8", 8, idx)
  }
}

resource "aws_vpc" "main" {
  for_each = { for d in local.deployments : "${d.env}-${d.region}" => d }

  cidr_block = local.vpc_cidrs["${each.value.env}-${each.value.region}"]

  tags = {
    Name        = "VPC-${each.value.env}-${each.value.region}"
    Environment = each.value.env
    Region      = each.value.region
    Continent   = each.value.continent
  }
}

resource "aws_instance" "app" {
  for_each = { for d in local.deployments : "${d.env}-${d.region}" => d }

  ami           = data.aws_ami.amazon_linux[each.value.region].id
  instance_type = local.instance_types[each.value.env][each.value.continent]
  subnet_id     = aws_subnet.main[each.key].id

  tags = {
    Name        = "App-${each.value.env}-${each.value.region}"
    Environment = each.value.env
    Region      = each.value.region
  }
}

data "aws_ami" "amazon_linux" {
  for_each = toset(flatten(values(local.regions)))

  owners      = ["amazon"]
  most_recent = true

  filter {
    name   = "name"
    values = ["amzn2-ami-hvm-*-x86_64-gp2"]
  }
}

output "vpc_cidrs" {
  value = local.vpc_cidrs
}

output "instance_ips" {
  value = {
    for key, instance in aws_instance.app : key => instance.private_ip
  }
}
```

This configuration demonstrates:

- Dynamic generation of deployment configurations using nested `for` expressions and `flatten`
- Use of `cidrsubnet` function for automatic CIDR block calculation
- Complex map and list manipulations to define infrastructure based on environment and region
- Dynamic resource creation using `for_each` with complex keys

Discussion

This approach showcases several advanced Terraform techniques:

Complex data transformations
    The use of nested `for` expressions and `flatten` allows for the creation of complex data structures that drive the configuration.

Dynamic CIDR allocation
    The `cidrsubnet` function is used to automatically calculate unique CIDR blocks for each VPC, eliminating the need for manual IP management.

Conditional resource attributes
    Instance types are determined dynamically based on both environment and geographic location.

Reusable data sources
    The AMI data source is created for each region, allowing for region-specific AMI selection.

Advanced resource creation
    The `for_each` meta-argument is used with a complex map to create resources, providing fine-grained control over resource creation.

Flexible outputs
    The outputs demonstrate how to create structured data from dynamically created resources.

When implementing these advanced techniques, consider:

Readability versus complexity
    While these techniques are powerful, they can make configurations harder to understand. Use comments and clear variable names to maintain readability.

Testing
    Complex expressions should be thoroughly tested. Use `terraform console` to validate your expressions before applying.

Performance

Very complex or large-scale use of these techniques can impact the Terraform life cycle times. Monitor performance and optimize where necessary.

Maintainability

Ensure that team members are familiar with these advanced techniques to maintain and extend the configuration.

State management

Be cautious when modifying expressions that affect resource addresses, as this could cause unexpected resource re-creation.

Modularization

Consider breaking down very complex configurations into smaller, focused modules for better manageability.

By leveraging these advanced functions and expressions, you can create highly dynamic and flexible Terraform configurations that adapt to complex infrastructure requirements while minimizing code duplication and manual configuration.

9.8 Integrating Terraform with Monitoring Tools

Problem

Setting up and maintaining self-hosted monitoring solutions can be complex and resource-intensive. There's a need for a more scalable, managed approach to monitoring and observability that integrates seamlessly with Terraform-managed infrastructure. Figure 9-1 illustrates a typical pipeline for setting up monitoring with IaC. This diagram shows how Terraform configurations can be used to provision and configure monitoring resources, such as dashboards, alerts, and data collection agents, alongside your infrastructure resources.

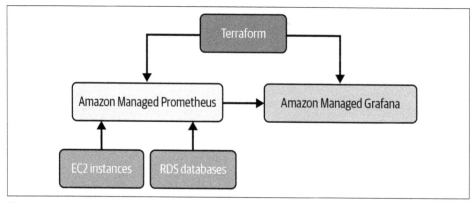

Figure 9-1. Setting up monitoring with IaC

Solution

This solution demonstrates how to use Terraform to set up and configure Amazon Managed Service for Prometheus (AMP) and Amazon Managed Grafana, integrating them with your AWS infrastructure:

```
# Set up Amazon Managed Service for Prometheus (AMP)
resource "aws_prometheus_workspace" "main" {
  alias = "my-prometheus-workspace"
}

# Set up Amazon Managed Grafana
resource "aws_grafana_workspace" "main" {
  account_access_type      = "CURRENT_ACCOUNT"
  authentication_providers = ["AWS_SSO"]
  permission_type          = "SERVICE_MANAGED"
  role_arn                 = aws_iam_role.grafana.arn
}

# IAM role for Grafana
resource "aws_iam_role" "grafana" {
  name = "managed-grafana-role"

  assume_role_policy = jsonencode({
    Version = "2012-10-17"
    Statement = [
      {
        Action = "sts:AssumeRole"
        Effect = "Allow"
        Principal = {
          Service = "grafana.amazonaws.com"
        }
      }
    ]
  })
}

# Policy to allow Grafana to access AMP
resource "aws_iam_role_policy" "grafana_amp_access" {
  name = "grafana-amp-access"
  role = aws_iam_role.grafana.id

  policy = jsonencode({
    Version = "2012-10-17"
    Statement = [
      {
        Effect = "Allow"
        Action = [
          "aps:QueryMetrics",
          "aps:GetLabels",
          "aps:GetSeries",
          "aps:GetMetricMetadata"
        ]
        Resource = aws_prometheus_workspace.main.arn
      }
    ]
  })
}

# VPC Endpoint for AMP (assuming you're using a VPC)
resource "aws_vpc_endpoint" "amp" {
  vpc_id          = var.vpc_id
```

```
  service_name       = "com.amazonaws.${var.region}.aps-workspaces"
  vpc_endpoint_type = "Interface"
  subnet_ids        = var.private_subnet_ids
  security_group_ids = [aws_security_group.amp_endpoint.id]
}

# Security group for AMP VPC Endpoint
resource "aws_security_group" "amp_endpoint" {
  name        = "amp-endpoint-sg"
  description = "Security group for AMP VPC Endpoint"
  vpc_id      = var.vpc_id

  ingress {
    from_port   = 443
    to_port     = 443
    protocol    = "tcp"
    cidr_blocks = [var.vpc_cidr]
  }
}

# Grafana-AMP Integration
resource "aws_grafana_workspace_api_key" "main" {
  key_name        = "amp-integration"
  key_role        = "VIEWER"
  seconds_to_live = 3600
  workspace_id    = aws_grafana_workspace.main.id
}

# Outputs
output "prometheus_endpoint" {
  value = aws_prometheus_workspace.main.prometheus_endpoint
}

output "grafana_endpoint" {
  value = aws_grafana_workspace.main.endpoint
}
```

This configuration:

- Sets up an Amazon Managed Service for Prometheus workspace
- Creates an Amazon Managed Grafana workspace
- Configures necessary IAM roles and policies for integration
- Sets up a VPC endpoint for secure access to AMP (assuming you're using a VPC)
- Creates an API key for Grafana-AMP integration

Discussion

This approach leverages AWS managed services for monitoring and observability, offering several advantages:

Scalability and reliability
  AWS-managed services automatically handle scaling and high availability.

Reduced operational overhead
  There is no need to manage and update Prometheus and Grafana servers.

Seamless integration

AMP and Managed Grafana are designed to work well with other AWS services.

Security

This utilizes AWS IAM for access control and VPC endpoints for secure communication.

Cost-effective

You pay for what you use, without the need to provision and manage dedicated instances.

When implementing this solution, consider:

Data ingestion

Set up Prometheus remote write from your applications or use AWS Distro for OpenTelemetry to send metrics to AMP.

Dashboard as code

While not shown here, consider using the Grafana provider to manage dashboards as code.

Cross-account monitoring

For large organizations, set up cross-account access to centralize monitoring.

Alerting

Configure alerting rules in AMP and integrate with Amazon SNS or other notification services.

Log integration

Consider integrating with CloudWatch logs for a complete observability solution.

Cost management

Monitor usage and set up budgets to keep costs under control.

Compliance

Ensure your monitoring setup meets any compliance requirements (e.g., data retention policies).

To extend this setup:

1. Add Prometheus remote write configurations to your applications.
2. Set up AWS Distro for OpenTelemetry collectors to gather metrics from various AWS services.
3. Create Grafana dashboards using Terraform or the Grafana API.
4. Implement alerting rules and notification channels.

By using AWS managed services for Prometheus and Grafana, you can create a scalable, reliable monitoring solution that integrates seamlessly with your Terraform-managed infrastructure, reducing operational overhead and improving your overall observability capabilities.

9.9 Managing Security and Compliance with Terraform

Problem

Maintaining security and compliance in dynamic, cloud-based infrastructures is challenging. Manual processes are error-prone and can't keep up with the pace of changes in modern environments.

Solution

This solution demonstrates advanced techniques for automating security and compliance checks using Terraform, integrating with tools such as AWS Config, HashiCorp Sentinel, and Open Policy Agent (OPA):

```
# Set up AWS Config
resource "aws_config_configuration_recorder" "main" {
  name     = "config-recorder"
  role_arn = aws_iam_role.config_role.arn

  recording_group {
    all_supported = true
    include_global_resource_types = true
  }
}

resource "aws_config_delivery_channel" "main" {
  name           = "config-delivery-channel"
  s3_bucket_name = aws_s3_bucket.config_logs.id
  sns_topic_arn  = aws_sns_topic.config_updates.arn

  depends_on = [aws_config_configuration_recorder.main]
}

# AWS Config Rules
resource "aws_config_config_rule" "s3_bucket_public_read_prohibited" {
  name = "s3-bucket-public-read-prohibited"

  source {
    owner             = "AWS"
    source_identifier = "S3_BUCKET_PUBLIC_READ_PROHIBITED"
  }
}

resource "aws_config_config_rule" "ec2_encrypted_volumes" {
  name = "ec2-encrypted-volumes"

  source {
    owner             = "AWS"
    source_identifier = "ENCRYPTED_VOLUMES"
  }
}
```

```
}

# IAM Role for AWS Config
resource "aws_iam_role" "config_role" {
  name = "aws-config-role"

  assume_role_policy = jsonencode({
    Version = "2012-10-17"
    Statement = [
      {
        Action = "sts:AssumeRole"
        Effect = "Allow"
        Principal = {
          Service = "config.amazonaws.com"
        }
      }
    ]
  })
}

resource "aws_iam_role_policy_attachment" "config_policy" {
  role       = aws_iam_role.config_role.name
  policy_arn = "arn:aws:iam::aws:policy/service-role/AWSConfigRole"
}

# S3 Bucket for Config Logs
resource "aws_s3_bucket" "config_logs" {
  bucket = "my-config-logs-bucket"
}

resource "aws_s3_bucket_policy" "config_logs" {
  bucket = aws_s3_bucket.config_logs.id
  policy = jsonencode({
    Version = "2012-10-17"
    Statement = [
      {
        Sid     = "AllowConfigWriteAccess"
        Effect = "Allow"
        Principal = {
          Service = "config.amazonaws.com"
        }
        Action = [
          "s3:PutObject"
        ]
        Resource = "${aws_s3_bucket.config_logs.arn}/*"
        Condition = {
          StringEquals = {
            "s3:x-amz-acl" = "bucket-owner-full-control"
          }
        }
      }
    ]
  })
}

# SNS Topic for Config Updates
resource "aws_sns_topic" "config_updates" {
  name = "config-updates-topic"
}

# Example of a custom Sentinel policy (normally stored in a separate .sentinel file)
# policy "restrict-ec2-instance-type" {
#   enforcement_level = "soft-mandatory"
#
```

```
#   main = rule {
#     all aws_instance as instance {
#       instance.instance_type in ["t3.micro", "t3.small", "t3.medium"]
#     }
#   }
# }

# Example of integrating OPA with Terraform using null_resource
resource "null_resource" "opa_check" {
  triggers = {
    always_run = "${timestamp()}"
  }

  provisioner "local-exec" {
    command = "opa eval --data policy.rego --input terraform.tfplan 'data.terraform.analysis.score'"
  }
}
```

This configuration:

1. Sets up AWS Config for continuous compliance monitoring

2. Defines AWS Config rules for S3 bucket public access and EC2 volume encryption

3. Creates necessary IAM roles and S3 bucket for AWS Config

4. Includes an example of a Sentinel policy (commented out as it's typically defined separately)

5. Demonstrates integration with OPA for policy evaluation

Discussion

This approach showcases several advanced techniques for automating security and compliance:

Continuous compliance monitoring
    AWS Config continuously evaluates your resources against defined rules, providing real-time compliance status.

Custom policy enforcement
    The Sentinel policy example (commented out) demonstrates how to enforce custom policies, such as restricting EC2 instance types.

Integration with external tools
    The OPA integration example shows how to incorporate third-party policy engines into your Terraform workflow.

Automated remediation
    While not shown in the code, AWS Config can be set up with auto-remediation actions for certain noncompliant resources.

Audit trail
    The S3 bucket and SNS topic set up for AWS Config provide a comprehensive audit trail of configuration changes and compliance status.

When implementing advanced security and compliance automation:

Policy as code
    Treat your security and compliance policies as code, versioning and reviewing them like any other code.

Layered approach
    Use a combination of cloud-native services (like AWS Config), infrastructure-as-code policies (Sentinel), and external tools (OPA) for comprehensive coverage.

Continuous validation
    Implement these checks in your CI/CD pipeline to catch issues before they reach production.

Least privilege
    Ensure that IAM roles and policies follow the principle of least privilege.

Encryption
    Implement encryption for data at rest and in transit. Consider using AWS KMS for key management.

Network security
    Implement VPC flow logs, security groups, and network access control lists (NACLs). Consider using AWS Network Firewall for advanced network protection.

Monitoring and alerting
    Set up alerts for compliance violations and security events. Integrate with your incident response system.

Regular reviews
    Periodically review and update your security policies to address new threats and compliance requirements.

Cross-account security
    For organizations with multiple AWS accounts, consider implementing AWS Organizations and AWS Control Tower for centralized governance.

By leveraging these advanced security and compliance automation techniques, you can create a robust, continuously monitored infrastructure that adheres to your organization's security policies and compliance requirements. This approach not only improves your security posture but also provides auditable evidence of compliance, crucial for regulated industries.

9.10 Advanced Debugging Techniques in Terraform

Problem

Complex Terraform configurations can lead to unexpected behaviors, resource conflicts, and difficult-to-trace errors, especially in large-scale, multimodule projects.

Solution

This solution demonstrates advanced debugging techniques for Terraform, including detailed logging, state manipulation, and targeted resource management:

```
# Enable detailed logging
# Run this before your Terraform commands:
# export TF_LOG=TRACE
# export TF_LOG_PATH=./terraform.log

# Example resource for demonstration
resource "aws_instance" "example" {
  ami           = "ami-0c55b159cbfafe1f0"
  instance_type = "t2.micro"
  tags = {
    Name = "DebugExample"
  }
}

# Output for debugging
output "instance_id" {
  value = aws_instance.example.id
}
```

Advanced debugging techniques:

- Detailed logging: set TF_LOG=TRACE and TF_LOG_PATH=./terraform.log before running Terraform commands.

- State inspection:

  ```
  terraform show
  terraform state list
  terraform state show aws_instance.example
  ```

- Plan analysis:

  ```
  terraform plan -out=tfplan
  terraform show -json tfplan | jq
  ```

- Targeted operations:

  ```
  terraform plan -target=aws_instance.example
  terraform apply -target=aws_instance.example
  ```

- Module inspection:

  ```
  terraform state pull | jq '.resources[] | select(.module
    == "module.example")'
  ```

- Refresh state:

```
terraform refresh
```

- Console for expression testing:

```
terraform console
> aws_instance.example.id
```

- Verbose provider debugging: set `TF_LOG_PROVIDER=DEBUG` for provider-specific logs.

Discussion

These advanced debugging techniques help tackle complex issues in Terraform configurations:

Detailed logging
Setting `TF_LOG=TRACE` provides comprehensive logs of Terraform's operations, API calls, and decision-making processes. This is crucial for understanding the root cause of errors or unexpected behaviors.

State inspection
The `terraform show` and `terraform state` commands allow you to inspect the current state, which is vital for understanding discrepancies between your configuration and the actual infrastructure.

Plan analysis
Outputting the plan to JSON and using tools such as `jq` allows for detailed analysis of planned changes, helping to catch potential issues before applying.

Targeted operations
Using the `-target` flag allows you to focus on specific resources, which is invaluable when debugging in large configurations or when you need to carefully manage dependencies.

Module inspection
For complex, multimodule setups, being able to inspect the state of specific modules helps in isolating issues.

Refresh state
The `terraform refresh` command updates the state file with the real-world infrastructure, helping to identify drift or manual changes.

Console for expression testing
The `terraform console` allows you to test expressions and functions interactively, which is extremely useful for debugging complex variable manipulations or data transformations.

Verbose provider debugging
> Provider-specific logging can help when the issue is related to provider API calls or behavior.

Additional considerations:

Version control
> Always use version control for your Terraform configurations. This allows you to track changes over time and revert if necessary.

Workspaces
> Use Terraform workspaces to isolate state between different environments, making it easier to debug environment-specific issues.

State backups
> Always back up your state file before performing any state manipulations.

Modular design
> Structure your Terraform code in modules. This not only improves reusability but also makes debugging easier by isolating functionality.

Custom validation rules
> Implement custom validation rules in your Terraform configurations to catch potential issues early.

External data sources
> When debugging issues related to external data sources, use `terraform refresh` to ensure you're working with the latest data.

CI/CD integration
> Integrate these debugging techniques into your CI/CD pipeline for automated issue detection.

By mastering these advanced debugging techniques, you can more effectively troubleshoot complex Terraform configurations, reducing downtime and improving the reliability of your infrastructure-as-code practices. Remember that effective debugging often requires a combination of these techniques, along with a systematic approach to isolating and resolving issues.

## CHAPTER 10

Real-World Use Cases

Let's explore a range of real-world use cases where Terraform excels in managing infrastructure as code. From orchestrating multiple environments to deploying highly available applications, we'll demonstrate how Terraform can solve complex infrastructure challenges across various cloud providers and tools.

Throughout these examples, we'll work with various cloud providers, primarily AWS, and explore integrations with tools like Kubernetes, AWS Lambda, and API Gateway. We'll also discuss advanced topics such as implementing GitOps workflows and automating disaster recovery to showcase Terraform's versatility in real-world scenarios.

By the end of this chapter, you'll have a solid understanding of how to apply Terraform to solve complex infrastructure challenges. You'll be equipped with practical examples, best practices, and the confidence to implement Terraform in your projects, enabling you to manage infrastructure as code efficiently and effectively across various environments and use cases.

10.1 Managing Multiple Environments with Terraform Workspaces

Problem

As organizations grow and their infrastructure complexity increases, managing multiple environments such as development, staging, and production becomes a significant challenge. Each environment may have different configurations, resources, and variables, leading to code duplication and increased maintenance efforts. Manually managing these environments can be error-prone and time-consuming.

Solution

Terraform provides a feature called workspaces that allows you to manage multiple environments within a single Terraform configuration. By leveraging workspaces, you can define different variables, resources, and configurations for each environment while keeping your Terraform code DRY (Don't Repeat Yourself):

```
# Define the workspace variable
variable "environment" {
  type = string
  default = terraform.workspace
}

# Configure the AWS provider
provider "aws" {
  region = var.region
}

# Define environment-specific variables
variable "instance_type" {
  type = map(string)
  default = {
    default = "t2.micro"
    dev     = "t2.small"
    prod    = "t2.medium"
  }
}

# Create an EC2 instance based on the workspace
resource "aws_instance" "example" {
  ami           = var.ami_id
  instance_type = var.instance_type[terraform.workspace]
  tags = {
    Name = "example-instance-${terraform.workspace}"
  }
}
```

To manage multiple environments, you can create separate workspaces for each environment:

```
$ terraform workspace new dev
$ terraform workspace new prd
```

Then, you can switch between workspaces using the terraform workspace select command:

```
$ terraform workspace select dev
$ terraform apply

$ terraform workspace select prd
$ terraform apply
```

Terraform will manage separate state files for each workspace, allowing you to maintain different resource configurations and variables for each environment.

Discussion

Terraform workspaces offer a powerful way to manage multiple environments within a single configuration, promoting code reusability and maintainability. By leveraging workspaces, you can define environment-specific configurations and variables, ensuring each environment is customized to its unique requirements while keeping the core infrastructure code consistent.

Key benefits of using Terraform workspaces for managing multiple environments include:

Code reusability
The same Terraform configuration can be used across different environments, reducing duplication and maintenance overhead.

Environment isolation
Each workspace maintains its own state file, ensuring that changes in one environment do not unintentionally impact others.

Simplified configuration management
Environment-specific variables can be easily defined and managed within the same configuration file.

Consistent workflow
The process for applying changes remains the same across all environments, reducing the risk of human error.

Version control friendly
A single set of Terraform files can be version-controlled, making it easier to track changes and collaborate across teams.

When implementing Terraform workspaces for multiple environments, consider the following best practices:

- Use clear and consistent naming conventions for workspaces, matching your environment names (e.g., development, staging, production).
- Implement a robust variable management strategy, using workspace-specific variable files or leveraging Terraform's built-in workspace name variable.
- Use conditional expressions to handle environment-specific resource configurations or counts.
- Implement proper access controls to ensure that only authorized team members can modify specific environments.
- Regularly review and update your workspace configurations to ensure they align with evolving infrastructure requirements.

By embracing Terraform workspaces, you can streamline the management of multiple environments, reduce the risk of configuration drift, and improve the overall efficiency of your infrastructure as code practices.

10.2 Deploying a Highly Available Web Application Across Regions

Problem

Ensuring high availability and fault tolerance is crucial for mission-critical web applications. Deploying an application in a single region makes it susceptible to outages and performance issues. The application would become unavailable in the event of a regional failure, leading to lost revenue and poor user experience. To mitigate these risks, deploying the application across multiple regions is essential. Figure 10-1 illustrates the architecture of a highly available web application deployed across multiple AWS regions.

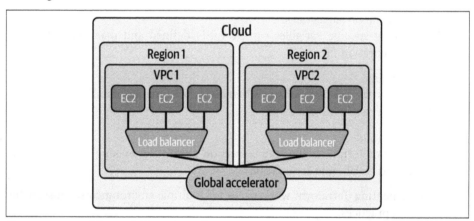

Figure 10-1. Highly available web application composition

Solution

Terraform enables you to deploy a highly available web application across multiple regions using a combination of resources and modules. This solution demonstrates how to provision resources in different regions and configure load balancing and failover mechanisms to ensure that your application remains available despite regional outages.

Here's an example of how to deploy a highly available web application across regions using Terraform:

```
# Configure the AWS provider for multiple regions
provider "aws" {
  alias  = "us_east_1"
  region = "us-east-1"
}

provider "aws" {
  alias  = "us_west_2"
```

```
  region = "us-west-2"
}

# Create a VPC in each region
module "vpc_east" {
  source = "./modules/vpc"
  providers = {
    aws = aws.us_east_1
  }
  cidr_block = "10.0.0.0/16"
  region     = "us-east-1"
}

module "vpc_west" {
  source = "./modules/vpc"
  providers = {
    aws = aws.us_west_2
  }
  cidr_block = "10.1.0.0/16"
  region     = "us-west-2"
}

# Create an Auto Scaling group in each region
module "asg_east" {
  source = "./modules/asg"
  providers = {
    aws = aws.us_east_1
  }
  vpc_id           = module.vpc_east.vpc_id
  subnet_ids       = module.vpc_east.public_subnet_ids
  min_size         = 2
  max_size         = 5
  desired_capacity = 2
  instance_type    = "t3.micro"
  app_name         = "example-app"
}

module "asg_west" {
  source = "./modules/asg"
  providers = {
    aws = aws.us_west_2
  }
  vpc_id           = module.vpc_west.vpc_id
  subnet_ids       = module.vpc_west.public_subnet_ids
  min_size         = 2
  max_size         = 5
  desired_capacity = 2
  instance_type    = "t3.micro"
  app_name         = "example-app"
}

# Create a global accelerator for high availability
resource "aws_globalaccelerator_accelerator" "example" {
  name            = "example-accelerator"
  ip_address_type = "IPV4"
  enabled         = true
}

# Create a listener for the global accelerator
resource "aws_globalaccelerator_listener" "example" {
  accelerator_arn = aws_globalaccelerator_accelerator.example.id
  client_affinity = "SOURCE_IP"
  protocol        = "TCP"
```

```
  port_range {
    from_port = 80
    to_port   = 80
  }
}

# Attach regional load balancers to the global accelerator
resource "aws_globalaccelerator_endpoint_group" "example" {
  listener_arn = aws_globalaccelerator_listener.example.id

  endpoint_configuration {
    endpoint_id = module.asg_east.alb_arn
    weight      = 50
  }

  endpoint_configuration {
    endpoint_id = module.asg_west.alb_arn
    weight      = 50
  }
}
```

This solution creates VPCs and Auto Scaling groups in two regions (us-east-1 and us-west-2) and uses AWS Global Accelerator to distribute traffic between the regions. The Global Accelerator provides a single entry point for your application and automatically routes traffic to the nearest healthy endpoint.

Discussion

Deploying a highly available web application across regions using Terraform offers several advantages:

Increased fault tolerance

By distributing the application across multiple regions, you ensure that it remains available even if an entire region experiences an outage. If one region goes down, traffic can be seamlessly redirected to the healthy region, minimizing downtime and maintaining business continuity.

Improved performance

Deploying the application closer to end users in different geographic locations can significantly improve latency and response times. The Global Accelerator routes traffic to the nearest available region, providing a better user experience.

Scalability and flexibility

Terraform allows you to define your infrastructure as code, making it easy to scale your application across regions. You can easily add or remove regions, adjust capacity, and update configurations using version-controlled Terraform code.

Disaster recovery

With a multiregion deployment, you have a built-in disaster recovery mechanism. If a region experiences a catastrophic failure, you can quickly failover to another region and restore service.

When implementing a multiregion deployment with Terraform, consider the following best practices:

- Use Terraform modules to encapsulate common configurations and promote code reusability across regions.
- Leverage Terraform's built-in support for multiple providers to manage resources in different regions seamlessly.
- Implement robust monitoring and alerting mechanisms to promptly detect and respond to regional outages.
- Regularly test your failover and disaster recovery processes to ensure they work as expected.
- Consider data replication and consistency requirements when designing your multiregion architecture.
- Use consistent tagging and naming conventions across regions to simplify management and monitoring.

By leveraging Terraform for multiregion deployments, you can create a robust, highly available infrastructure that ensures your application remains accessible and performant for users around the globe.

10.3 Provisioning a Scalable Kubernetes Cluster on AWS EKS

Problem

Kubernetes has become the de facto standard for container orchestration, but deploying a scalable Kubernetes cluster can be a complex and time-consuming task. Manually provisioning and configuring the underlying infrastructure, setting up the control plane, and managing worker nodes can be challenging, especially when it comes to ensuring high availability, security, and scalability.

Solution

Terraform provides a streamlined way to provision a scalable Kubernetes cluster on AWS using the EKS. This solution demonstrates how to use Terraform to define your entire Kubernetes infrastructure as code, including the EKS cluster, worker nodes, networking, and security configurations.

Here's an example of how to provision a scalable Kubernetes cluster on AWS EKS using Terraform:

```
# Configure the AWS provider
provider "aws" {
  region = "us-west-2"
}

# Create a VPC for the EKS cluster
module "vpc" {
  source  = "terraform-aws-modules/vpc/aws"
  version = "3.14.0"

  name = "eks-vpc"
  cidr = "10.0.0.0/16"

  azs             = ["us-west-2a", "us-west-2b", "us-west-2c"]
  private_subnets = ["10.0.1.0/24", "10.0.2.0/24", "10.0.3.0/24"]
  public_subnets  = ["10.0.101.0/24", "10.0.102.0/24", "10.0.103.0/24"]

  enable_nat_gateway = true
  single_nat_gateway = true

  tags = {
    "kubernetes.io/cluster/my-eks-cluster" = "shared"
  }
}

# Create an EKS cluster
module "eks" {
  source  = "terraform-aws-modules/eks/aws"
  version = "20.24.0"

  cluster_name    = "my-eks-cluster"
  cluster_version = "1.24"

  vpc_id     = module.vpc.vpc_id
  subnet_ids = module.vpc.private_subnets

  eks_managed_node_groups = {
    general = {
      desired_size = 2
      min_size     = 1
      max_size     = 4

      instance_types = ["t3.medium"]
      capacity_type  = "ON_DEMAND"
    }
  }

  tags = {
    Environment = "production"
    Application = "my-app"
  }
}

# Output the kubectl configuration
output "kubectl_config" {
  description = "kubectl config to access the EKS cluster"
  value       = module.eks.kubeconfig
  sensitive   = true
}
```

Discussion

Provisioning a scalable Kubernetes cluster on AWS EKS using Terraform offers several benefits:

Infrastructure as code
By defining your entire EKS infrastructure in Terraform, you gain the advantages of version control, collaboration, and reproducibility. This approach ensures that your infrastructure is consistent, reliable, and easily maintainable.

Simplified cluster management
Terraform abstracts away much of the complexity involved in setting up an EKS cluster, handling tasks such as VPC configuration, IAM role creation, and worker node provisioning.

Scalability
With just a few lines of code, you can adjust the desired number of worker nodes, enabling your cluster to adapt to changing workload demands. This scalability allows you to optimize resource utilization and cost-effectiveness without compromising performance.

Integration with AWS services
Terraform's AWS provider allows seamless integration with other AWS services, making it easy to set up additional resources such as load balancers, databases, or storage solutions that your Kubernetes applications might require.

Customization and flexibility
The modular approach used in this example allows for easy customization. You can adjust node instance types, cluster version, VPC configuration, and other parameters to meet your specific requirements.

When implementing an EKS cluster with Terraform, consider the following best practices:

- Use Terraform modules (as demonstrated in the example) to encapsulate and reuse common configurations.

- Implement proper networking and security configurations, including private subnets for worker nodes and appropriate security groups.

- Utilize EKS managed node groups for simplified node management and automatic updates.

- Configure cluster autoscaling to automatically adjust the number of worker nodes based on demand.

- Implement proper IAM roles and policies to ensure the principle of least privilege.

- Use Terraform workspaces or separate state files to manage multiple environments (e.g., development, staging, production).
- Regularly update your EKS cluster and node groups to benefit from the latest features and security patches.

By leveraging Terraform for EKS cluster provisioning, you can streamline your Kubernetes deployment process, ensure consistency across environments, and focus on developing and deploying your applications rather than managing the underlying infrastructure.

10.4 Implementing Blue-Green Deployments with Terraform

Problem

Deploying new versions of applications can be challenging and risky. Traditional deployment methods often involve downtime, which can impact user experience and business operations. Additionally, rolling back to a previous version in case of issues can be complex and time-consuming. Blue-green deployments provide a solution to these challenges by allowing seamless transitions between different versions of an application.

Solution

Terraform can be used to implement blue-green deployments, enabling smooth and controlled transitions between application versions. This solution demonstrates how to create and manage the infrastructure required for blue-green deployments using Terraform's declarative approach and resource management capabilities.

Here's an example of how to implement blue-green deployments using Terraform and AWS:

```
# Configure the AWS provider
provider "aws" {
  region = "us-west-2"
}

# Create a VPC for the deployment
module "vpc" {
  source = "terraform-aws-modules/vpc/aws"

  name = "blue-green-vpc"
  cidr = "10.0.0.0/16"

  azs             = ["us-west-2a", "us-west-2b"]
  private_subnets = ["10.0.1.0/24", "10.0.2.0/24"]
  public_subnets  = ["10.0.101.0/24", "10.0.102.0/24"]

  enable_nat_gateway = true
```

```
  single_nat_gateway = true
}

# Create security group for the instances
resource "aws_security_group" "app_sg" {
  name        = "app-sg"
  description = "Security group for application instances"
  vpc_id      = module.vpc.vpc_id

  ingress {
    from_port   = 80
    to_port     = 80
    protocol    = "tcp"
    cidr_blocks = ["0.0.0.0/0"]
  }

  egress {
    from_port   = 0
    to_port     = 0
    protocol    = "-1"
    cidr_blocks = ["0.0.0.0/0"]
  }
}

# Create launch template for blue environment
resource "aws_launch_template" "blue" {
  name_prefix   = "blue-"
  image_id      = "ami-0c55b159cbfafe1f0"  # Replace with your AMI ID
  instance_type = "t3.micro"

  vpc_security_group_ids = [aws_security_group.app_sg.id]

  tag_specifications {
    resource_type = "instance"
    tags = {
      Name = "blue-instance"
    }
  }

  user_data = base64encode(<<-EOF
              #!/bin/bash
              echo "Hello from Blue Environment" > index.html
              nohup python -m SimpleHTTPServer 80 &
              EOF
  )
}

# Create launch template for green environment
resource "aws_launch_template" "green" {
  name_prefix   = "green-"
  image_id      = "ami-0c55b159cbfafe1f0"  # Replace with your AMI ID
  instance_type = "t3.micro"

  vpc_security_group_ids = [aws_security_group.app_sg.id]

  tag_specifications {
    resource_type = "instance"
    tags = {
      Name = "green-instance"
    }
  }

  user_data = base64encode(<<-EOF
              #!/bin/bash
```

```
                echo "Hello from Green Environment" > index.html
                nohup python -m SimpleHTTPServer 80 &
                EOF
    )
}

# Create Auto Scaling group for blue environment
resource "aws_autoscaling_group" "blue" {
  name                = "blue-asg"
  vpc_zone_identifier = module.vpc.private_subnets
  desired_capacity    = 2
  max_size            = 4
  min_size            = 1

  launch_template {
    id      = aws_launch_template.blue.id
    version = "$Latest"
  }

  target_group_arns = [aws_lb_target_group.blue.arn]
}

# Create Auto Scaling group for green environment
resource "aws_autoscaling_group" "green" {
  name                = "green-asg"
  vpc_zone_identifier = module.vpc.private_subnets
  desired_capacity    = 2
  max_size            = 4
  min_size            = 1

  launch_template {
    id      = aws_launch_template.green.id
    version = "$Latest"
  }

  target_group_arns = [aws_lb_target_group.green.arn]
}

# Create Application Load Balancer
resource "aws_lb" "app_lb" {
  name               = "app-lb"
  internal           = false
  load_balancer_type = "application"
  security_groups    = [aws_security_group.app_sg.id]
  subnets            = module.vpc.public_subnets
}

# Create target group for blue environment
resource "aws_lb_target_group" "blue" {
  name     = "blue-tg"
  port     = 80
  protocol = "HTTP"
  vpc_id   = module.vpc.vpc_id
}

# Create target group for green environment
resource "aws_lb_target_group" "green" {
  name     = "green-tg"
  port     = 80
  protocol = "HTTP"
  vpc_id   = module.vpc.vpc_id
}

# Create listener rule for blue-green deployment
```

```
resource "aws_lb_listener" "front_end" {
  load_balancer_arn = aws_lb.app_lb.arn
  port              = "80"
  protocol          = "HTTP"

  default_action {
    type = "forward"
    target_group_arn = aws_lb_target_group.blue.arn
  }
}

# Output the load balancer DNS name
output "lb_dns_name" {
  description = "The DNS name of the load balancer"
  value       = aws_lb.app_lb.dns_name
}
```

To switch between blue and green environments, you would update the `aws_lb_listener.front_end` resource to point to the desired target group.

Discussion

Implementing blue-green deployments with Terraform offers several benefits:

Zero-downtime deployments
> By creating separate environments (blue and green) and using a load balancer to route traffic, you can deploy new versions of your application without causing downtime.

Easy rollbacks
> If issues are detected in the new version, you can quickly roll back to the previous version by simply updating the load balancer configuration.

Testing in production-like environment
> The green environment allows you to test the new version in a production-like setting before directing live traffic to it.

Gradual traffic shift
> You can implement gradual traffic shifting between blue and green environments to minimize the impact of potential issues.

Infrastructure as code
> Defining your blue-green deployment infrastructure in Terraform ensures consistency and reproducibility across environments and deployments.

When implementing blue-green deployments with Terraform, consider the following best practices:

- Use Terraform modules to encapsulate the blue-green deployment logic, making it reusable across different applications or services.

- Implement proper health checks and monitoring to ensure the new environment is healthy before switching traffic.

- Automate the deployment process by integrating Terraform with your CI/CD pipeline.

- Consider using Terraform workspaces or separate state files to manage different stages of your blue-green deployment (e.g., staging, production).

- Implement proper access controls and security measures to protect both environments.

- Plan for data migration or synchronization between blue and green environments, especially for stateful applications.

- Regularly clean up unused resources to optimize costs, particularly after successful deployments when the old environment is no longer needed.

By leveraging Terraform for blue-green deployments, you can achieve more reliable and less risky application updates, improving your overall deployment process and application availability.

10.5 Automating Database Migrations with Terraform and AWS RDS

Problem

Managing database migrations can be a complex and error-prone process, especially when dealing with multiple environments and versions. Manually applying database schema changes and tracking migration history can lead to inconsistencies and deployment issues. Automating database migrations ensures that the database schema evolves in a controlled and repeatable manner, reducing the risk of data loss or inconsistencies.

Solution

Terraform can be used in conjunction with AWS Relational Database Service (RDS) to automate database migrations. This solution demonstrates how to leverage Terraform's declarative approach and AWS RDS's managed database capabilities to define and manage your database schema as code, ensuring consistent and reliable migrations across environments.

Here's an example of how to automate database migrations using Terraform and AWS RDS:

```
# Configure the AWS provider
provider "aws" {
  region = "us-west-2"
```

```
}

# Create an RDS instance
resource "aws_db_instance" "example" {
  identifier        = "example-db"
  engine            = "mysql"
  engine_version    = "8.0"
  instance_class    = "db.t3.micro"
  allocated_storage = 20
  db_name           = "myapp"
  username          = var.db_username
  password          = var.db_password

  vpc_security_group_ids = [aws_security_group.db_sg.id]
  db_subnet_group_name   = aws_db_subnet_group.example.name

  skip_final_snapshot = true
}

# Create a security group for the RDS instance
resource "aws_security_group" "db_sg" {
  name        = "db-sg"
  description = "Security group for RDS instance"
  vpc_id      = var.vpc_id

  ingress {
    from_port   = 3306
    to_port     = 3306
    protocol    = "tcp"
    cidr_blocks = ["10.0.0.0/16"]  # Adjust this to your VPC CIDR
  }
}

# Create a DB subnet group
resource "aws_db_subnet_group" "example" {
  name       = "example-db-subnet-group"
  subnet_ids = var.subnet_ids
}

# Define the database migration script
data "template_file" "migration_script" {
  template = file("${path.module}/migrations/V1__initial_schema.sql")
}

# Execute the migration script
resource "null_resource" "db_migration" {
  triggers = {
    migration_hash = sha256(data.template_file.migration_script.rendered)
  }

  provisioner "local-exec" {
    command = <<EOF
      mysql -h ${aws_db_instance.example.endpoint} -u ${var.db_username} -p${var.db_password}
        ${aws_db_instance.example.db_name} < ${path.module}/migrations/V1__initial_schema.sql
    EOF
  }

  depends_on = [aws_db_instance.example]
}

# Output the database endpoint
output "db_endpoint" {
  value = aws_db_instance.example.endpoint
}
```

To use this configuration:

1. Create a migrations directory in your Terraform project.

2. Add your SQL migration scripts to the migrations directory (e.g., `V1__ini tial_schema.sql`).

3. Run `terraform init` and `terraform apply` to create the RDS instance and execute the migration.

Discussion

Automating database migrations with Terraform and AWS RDS offers several benefits:

Version control
Database schema changes are version-controlled alongside your application code, providing a clear history of changes and making it easier to track and audit modifications.

Consistency across environments
By defining migrations as code, you ensure that the same schema changes are applied consistently across all environments (development, staging, production).

Repeatable process
Terraform's declarative approach allows you to create a repeatable process for applying migrations, reducing the risk of human error.

Integration with infrastructure provisioning
By combining database migrations with infrastructure provisioning, you can ensure that your database schema is always in sync with your application code.

Rollback capability
In case of issues, you can easily roll back to a previous version of your schema by applying the corresponding migration script.

When implementing automated database migrations with Terraform and AWS RDS, consider the following best practices:

Use a migration naming convention
Adopt a consistent naming convention for your migration scripts (e.g., `V1__description.sql`, `V2__description.sql`) to ensure they are applied in the correct order.

Idempotent migrations
Design your migration scripts to be idempotent, meaning that they can be run multiple times without causing errors or unintended changes.

Separate migration logic
Keep your migration scripts separate from your application code to maintain a clear separation of concerns.

Use Terraform workspaces
Leverage Terraform workspaces to manage migrations across different environments (development, staging, production).

Secure credentials
Use Terraform variables or AWS Secrets Manager to securely manage database credentials, avoiding hardcoded values in your Terraform configuration.

Test migrations
Always test your migrations in a nonproduction environment before applying them to production.

Backup strategy
Implement a robust backup strategy for your RDS instances to protect against data loss during migrations.

Monitor migration execution
Implement logging and monitoring for your migration process to quickly identify and troubleshoot any issues.

By leveraging Terraform and AWS RDS for database migrations, you can create a more reliable, repeatable, and manageable process for evolving your database schema alongside your application infrastructure.

10.6 Deploying a Serverless Application on AWS Lambda and API Gateway

Problem

Deploying serverless applications can be challenging, especially when it comes to managing the underlying infrastructure and integrating various services. Manually setting up AWS Lambda functions, configuring API Gateway, and managing permissions and triggers can be time-consuming and error-prone. Automating the deployment process ensures consistency, repeatability, and easier management of serverless applications.

Solution

Terraform provides a way to automate the deployment of serverless applications on AWS Lambda and API Gateway. This solution demonstrates how to use Terraform to define and deploy a serverless application, including the Lambda function, API Gateway, and necessary IAM roles and permissions.

Here's an example of how to deploy a serverless application using Terraform:

```
# Configure the AWS provider
provider "aws" {
  region = "us-west-2"
}

# Create an IAM role for the Lambda function
resource "aws_iam_role" "lambda_exec" {
  name = "serverless_lambda_role"

  assume_role_policy = jsonencode({
    Version = "2012-10-17"
    Statement = [{
      Action = "sts:AssumeRole"
      Effect = "Allow"
      Principal = {
        Service = "lambda.amazonaws.com"
      }
    }]
  })
}

# Attach necessary permissions to the Lambda role
resource "aws_iam_role_policy_attachment" "lambda_policy" {
  policy_arn = "arn:aws:iam::aws:policy/service-role/AWSLambdaBasicExecutionRole"
  role       = aws_iam_role.lambda_exec.name
}

# Create a Lambda function
resource "aws_lambda_function" "example" {
  filename      = "lambda_function.zip"
  function_name = "example_lambda_function"
  role          = aws_iam_role.lambda_exec.arn
  handler       = "index.handler"
  runtime       = "nodejs14.x"

  source_code_hash = filebase64sha256("lambda_function.zip")
}

# Create an API Gateway REST API
resource "aws_api_gateway_rest_api" "example" {
  name        = "example_api"
  description = "Example API Gateway REST API"
}

# Create an API Gateway resource
resource "aws_api_gateway_resource" "example" {
  rest_api_id = aws_api_gateway_rest_api.example.id
  parent_id   = aws_api_gateway_rest_api.example.root_resource_id
  path_part   = "example"
}

# Create an API Gateway method
resource "aws_api_gateway_method" "example" {
  rest_api_id   = aws_api_gateway_rest_api.example.id
  resource_id   = aws_api_gateway_resource.example.id
  http_method   = "GET"
  authorization = "NONE"
}
```

```
# Create an API Gateway integration
resource "aws_api_gateway_integration" "example" {
  rest_api_id             = aws_api_gateway_rest_api.example.id
  resource_id             = aws_api_gateway_resource.example.id
  http_method             = aws_api_gateway_method.example.http_method
  integration_http_method = "POST"
  type                    = "AWS_PROXY"
  uri                     = aws_lambda_function.example.invoke_arn
}

# Create an API Gateway deployment
resource "aws_api_gateway_deployment" "example" {
  depends_on = [aws_api_gateway_integration.example]

  rest_api_id = aws_api_gateway_rest_api.example.id
  stage_name  = "prod"
}

# Allow API Gateway to invoke the Lambda function
resource "aws_lambda_permission" "apigw_lambda" {
  statement_id  = "AllowExecutionFromAPIGateway"
  action        = "lambda:InvokeFunction"
  function_name = aws_lambda_function.example.function_name
  principal     = "apigateway.amazonaws.com"

  source_arn = "${aws_api_gateway_rest_api.example.execution_arn}/*/$
    {aws_api_gateway_method.example.http_method}${aws_api_gateway_resource.example.path}"
}

# Output the API Gateway URL
output "api_url" {
  value = "${aws_api_gateway_deployment.example.invoke_url}${aws_api_gateway_resource.example.path}"
}
```

To use this configuration:

1. Create a *lambda_function.zip* file containing your Lambda function code.

2. Run `terraform init` and `terraform apply` to deploy the serverless application.

Discussion

Deploying serverless applications with Terraform on AWS Lambda and API Gateway offers several benefits:

Infrastructure as code
> By defining your serverless infrastructure in Terraform, you gain version control, reproducibility, and easier collaboration among team members.

Automated deployments
> Terraform automates the process of creating and updating Lambda functions, API Gateway resources, and IAM roles, reducing manual errors and saving time.

Consistent environments
> You can use the same Terraform configuration to deploy your serverless application across different environments (development, staging, production), ensuring consistency.

Easy updates and rollbacks
> Terraform's state management makes it easy to update your serverless application or roll back to a previous version if needed.

Integration with other AWS services
> Terraform allows you to easily integrate your serverless application with other AWS services, such as DynamoDB, S3, or CloudWatch.

When implementing serverless applications with Terraform, consider the following best practices:

Use Terraform workspaces
> Leverage workspaces to manage different environments (development, staging, production) using the same Terraform configuration.

Modularize your configuration
> Break down your Terraform configuration into reusable modules for common components such as Lambda functions or API Gateway resources.

Manage function code separately
> Store your Lambda function code in a separate repository and use a CI/CD pipeline to package and upload it to S3 before Terraform deployment.

Use remote state
> Store your Terraform state file remotely (e.g., in an S3 bucket) to enable team collaboration and prevent state file conflicts.

Implement proper IAM permissions
> Follow the principle of least privilege when defining IAM roles and policies for your Lambda functions.

Configure logging and monitoring
> Set up CloudWatch logs and alarms to monitor your serverless application's performance and errors.

Use variables and locals
> Leverage Terraform variables and locals to make your configuration more flexible and easier to maintain.

Implement API versioning
> Use API Gateway stage variables or Lambda aliases to implement API versioning and enable gradual rollouts of new features.

By using Terraform to deploy serverless applications on AWS Lambda and API Gateway, you can create a more manageable, scalable, and reproducible infrastructure for your serverless workloads.

10.7 Implementing Infrastructure as Code for GitOps Workflows

Problem

Organizations often struggle with managing infrastructure across multiple environments (development, staging, production) while ensuring consistency, traceability, and automation. Traditional methods can lead to environment drift, manual errors, and difficulties in tracking changes across different stages of the deployment pipeline.

Solution

We can use Terraform and GitHub Actions to implement a multienvironment infrastructure deployment pipeline. This solution demonstrates how to set up a GitOps-style workflow that automatically plans and applies infrastructure changes to different environments based on Git branches.

Here's an example of how to implement this solution:

1. First, structure your Terraform configuration to support multiple environments:

   ```
   # environments/main.tf

   locals {
     environment = terraform.workspace
   }

   module "network" {
     source      = "../modules/network"
     environment = local.environment
   }

   module "compute" {
     source      = "../modules/compute"
     environment = local.environment
   }

   # Add more modules as needed
   ```

2. Create a *.github/workflows/terraform.yml* file in your repository:

   ```
   name: 'Terraform CI/CD'

   on:
     push:
       branches:
         - main
         - staging
         - development
   ```

```
    pull_request:
      branches: [ main ]

jobs:
  terraform:
    name: 'Terraform'
    runs-on: ubuntu-latest
    env:
      AWS_ACCESS_KEY_ID: ${{ secrets.AWS_ACCESS_KEY_ID }}
      AWS_SECRET_ACCESS_KEY: ${{ secrets.AWS_SECRET_ACCESS_KEY }}

    steps:
    - name: Checkout
      uses: actions/checkout@v2

    - name: Setup Terraform
      uses: hashicorp/setup-terraform@v1

    - name: Terraform Init
      run: terraform init
      working-directory: ./environments

    - name: Terraform Format
      run: terraform fmt -check
      working-directory: ./environments

    - name: Terraform Plan
      run: |
        terraform workspace select ${GITHUB_REF##*/} || terraform workspace new ${GITHUB_REF##*/}
        terraform plan -no-color
      working-directory: ./environments

    - name: Terraform Apply
      if: github.ref == 'refs/heads/main' && github.event_name == 'push'
      run: terraform apply -auto-approve
      working-directory: ./environments
```

3. Set up branch protection rules in GitHub to require pull request reviews before merging to the main branch.

4. Store your AWS credentials as GitHub Secrets (AWS_ACCESS_KEY_ID and AWS_SECRET_ACCESS_KEY).

5. Commit and push these files to your Git repository.

Now, when changes are pushed to any of the specified branches (development, staging, main), the GitHub Actions workflow will automatically run Terraform plans. Changes to the main branch will also trigger an automatic apply, while other branches require manual approval.

Discussion

Implementing multienvironment infrastructure deployment with Terraform and GitHub Actions offers several advantages:

Environment consistency

By using the same Terraform configurations across environments, you ensure consistency and reduce the risk of environment-specific issues.

Automated workflow

The GitHub Actions workflow automates the process of planning and applying changes, reducing manual intervention and potential errors.

Environment isolation

Using Terraform workspaces allows you to maintain separate state files for each environment, preventing unintended cross-environment modifications.

Change traceability

All infrastructure changes are tracked in Git, providing a clear history and enabling easy audits.

Controlled promotions

Changes can be tested in lower environments before being promoted to production, following the Git branch structure.

Pull request reviews

The pull request process allows for code reviews of infrastructure changes before they are applied.

When implementing this approach, consider the following best practices:

Use consistent naming

Adopt a consistent naming convention for resources across environments, possibly including the environment name as a prefix or suffix.

Parameterize environment-specific values

Use Terraform variables to manage values that differ between environments.

Implement strong access controls

Ensure that GitHub repository access and AWS IAM permissions are properly configured to maintain security.

Regular state cleanup

Periodically review and clean up old workspaces to manage Terraform state effectively.

Implement drift detection

Regularly run Terraform plan on all environments to detect and address any manual changes or drift.

Optimize for cost

Be mindful of costs associated with running multiple environments and consider using cheaper instance types or reducing resource counts in nonproduction environments.

By leveraging Terraform with GitHub Actions, teams can achieve a streamlined, automated, and version-controlled approach to managing infrastructure across multiple environments, aligning closely with GitOps principles and modern DevOps practices.

10.8 Optimizing Costs with Terraform and Spot Instances

Problem

Running infrastructure on cloud platforms can be expensive, especially when using on-demand instances for workloads that don't require constant availability. Organizations need to balance performance requirements with cost-efficiency, but managing a mix of instance types and pricing models can be complex and time-consuming.

Solution

Terraform can be used to automate the provisioning and management of AWS Spot Instances, enabling you to optimize costs while maintaining the desired level of availability and performance. This solution demonstrates how to use Terraform to create an Auto Scaling group that utilizes a mix of On-Demand and Spot Instances.

Here's an example of how to implement cost optimization using Terraform and AWS Spot Instances:

```
provider "aws" {
  region = "us-west-2"
}

resource "aws_launch_template" "example" {
  name_prefix   = "example-template"
  image_id      = "ami-0c55b159cbfafe1f0" # Amazon Linux 2 AMI (adjust as needed)
  instance_type = "t3.micro"

  # Add other configuration as needed (security groups, IAM instance profile, etc.)
}

resource "aws_autoscaling_group" "example" {
  name                 = "example-asg"
  vpc_zone_identifier  = ["subnet-12345678", "subnet-87654321"]
  min_size             = 2
  max_size             = 10
  desired_capacity     = 4

  mixed_instances_policy {
    launch_template {
      launch_template_specification {
        launch_template_id = aws_launch_template.example.id
        version            = "$Latest"
      }
```

```
    override {
      instance_type     = "t3.micro"
      weighted_capacity = "1"
    }
    override {
      instance_type     = "t3.small"
      weighted_capacity = "2"
    }
  }

  instances_distribution {
    on_demand_base_capacity                  = 1
    on_demand_percentage_above_base_capacity = 25
    spot_allocation_strategy                 = "capacity-optimized"
  }
}

tag {
  key                 = "Name"
  value               = "ASG-Instance"
  propagate_at_launch = true
}
}
```

Discussion

Optimizing costs with Terraform and Spot Instances offers several benefits:

Cost savings
> By leveraging Spot Instances, you can significantly reduce your infrastructure costs compared to using only On-Demand Instances.

Automated management
> Terraform automates the process of creating and managing Auto Scaling groups with mixed instance types, reducing manual effort and potential errors.

Flexibility
> The mixed instances policy allows you to define a variety of instance types, enabling your workload to run on whatever instance types are most cost-effective at any given time.

Availability
> By maintaining a base capacity of On-Demand Instances and using capacity-optimized allocation for Spot Instances, you can balance cost savings with application availability.

Scalability
> The Auto Scaling group automatically adjusts the number of instances based on demand, ensuring performance while optimizing costs.

When implementing cost optimization with Terraform and Spot Instances, consider the following best practices:

Instance diversity
> Use a mix of instance types and sizes to increase the likelihood of getting Spot Instances and to improve application resilience.

Spot Instance handling
> Design your application to be fault-tolerant and able to handle Spot Instance interruptions gracefully.

Monitoring and alerting
> Implement CloudWatch alarms to monitor your Auto Scaling group and alert on any capacity issues.

Regular review
> Periodically review your instance type selections and On-Demand/Spot mix to ensure they still align with your performance needs and cost goals.

Use Spot Instance data feed
> Enable the Spot Instance data feed to gain insights into Spot Instance usage and savings.

Implement Spot Instance termination notices
> Use the two-minute Spot Instance termination notice to gracefully handle instance terminations.

Consider Reserved Instances
> For predictable, long-term workloads, consider using a mix of Reserved Instances, On-Demand, and Spot Instances for optimal cost savings.

Use Auto Scaling group metrics
> Enable group metrics to get detailed insights into your Auto Scaling group's performance and cost efficiency.

By leveraging Terraform to manage a cost-optimized infrastructure with Spot Instances, you can achieve significant cost savings while maintaining the flexibility and scalability needed for your applications.

10.9 Deploying a Multicloud Monitoring Solution with Terraform

Problem

As organizations adopt multicloud strategies, monitoring the health and performance of resources across different cloud platforms becomes increasingly challenging. Each cloud provider offers its own monitoring tools and APIs, making it difficult to consolidate and centralize monitoring data. Manually configuring and managing monitoring solutions for each cloud platform can be time-consuming and error-prone.

Solution

Terraform provides a way to automate the deployment and configuration of multicloud monitoring solutions. By leveraging Terraform's provider ecosystem and cross-platform capabilities, you can deploy a centralized monitoring solution that aggregates data from multiple cloud platforms.

Here's an example of how to implement a multicloud monitoring solution using Terraform, AWS, Azure, and Datadog:

```
# Configure providers
provider "aws" {
  region = "us-west-2"
}

provider "azurerm" {
  features {}
}

provider "datadog" {
  api_key = var.datadog_api_key
  app_key = var.datadog_app_key
}

# Deploy AWS resources
resource "aws_instance" "example" {
  ami           = "ami-0c55b159cbfafe1f0"
  instance_type = "t3.micro"

  tags = {
    Name = "example-aws-instance"
  }
}

# Deploy Azure resources
resource "azurerm_resource_group" "example" {
  name     = "example-resources"
  location = "East US"
}

resource "azurerm_virtual_machine" "example" {
  name                  = "example-vm"
  location              = azurerm_resource_group.example.location
  resource_group_name   = azurerm_resource_group.example.name
  network_interface_ids = [azurerm_network_interface.example.id]
  vm_size               = "Standard_DS1_v2"

  # Add OS and storage configuration here
}

# Configure Datadog monitors
resource "datadog_monitor" "aws_cpu" {
  name    = "High CPU Usage - AWS"
  type    = "metric alert"
  message = "CPU usage is high on AWS instance {{host.name}}."
```

```
  query   = "avg(last_5m):avg:aws.ec2.cpu{host:${aws_instance.example.id}} > 80"

  monitor_thresholds {
    critical = 80
  }
}

resource "datadog_monitor" "azure_cpu" {
  name    = "High CPU Usage - Azure"
  type    = "metric alert"
  message = "CPU usage is high on Azure VM {{host.name}}."
  query   = "avg(last_5m):avg:azure.vm.percentage_cpu{resource_group:${azurerm_resource_group.example.
    name},name:${azurerm_virtual_machine.example.name}} > 80"

  monitor_thresholds {
    critical = 80
  }
}

# Output the Datadog dashboard URL
resource "datadog_dashboard" "multi_cloud" {
  title       = "Multi-Cloud Overview"
  description = "Overview of AWS and Azure resources"
  layout_type = "ordered"

  widget {
    timeseries_definition {
      title = "CPU Usage - AWS vs Azure"
      request {
        q   = "avg:aws.ec2.cpu{host:${aws_instance.example.id}}"
        display_type = "line"
      }
      request {
        q   = "avg:azure.vm.percentage_cpu{resource_group:$
          {azurerm_resource_group.example.name},name:${azurerm_virtual_machine.example.name}}"
        display_type = "line"
      }
    }
  }
}

output "datadog_dashboard_url" {
  value = "https://app.datadoghq.com/dashboard/${datadog_dashboard.multi_cloud.id}"
}
```

Discussion

Deploying a multicloud monitoring solution with Terraform offers several benefits:

Centralized monitoring

> By using a third-party service such as Datadog, you can aggregate monitoring data from multiple cloud providers into a single pane of glass.

Consistency

> Terraform ensures that monitoring configurations are consistent across different cloud platforms and environments.

Automation

The entire process of provisioning resources and setting up monitoring is automated, reducing manual effort and potential for errors.

Version control

Monitoring configurations can be version-controlled alongside infrastructure code, providing a complete history of changes.

Scalability

As your multicloud infrastructure grows, Terraform makes it easy to add new resources and corresponding monitoring configurations.

When implementing a multicloud monitoring solution with Terraform, consider the following best practices:

Use variables

Leverage Terraform variables to make your configuration more flexible and reusable across different environments.

Modularize

Create separate Terraform modules for each cloud provider and for monitoring configurations to improve code organization and reusability.

Implement tagging strategy

Use consistent tagging across cloud providers to make it easier to organize and filter resources in your monitoring solution.

Secure credentials

Use secure methods to manage and inject credentials for cloud providers and monitoring services, such as environment variables or a secrets management system.

Monitor costs

Keep an eye on the costs associated with multicloud deployments and the chosen monitoring solution. Consider implementing cost allocation tags.

Get regular updates

Keep your Terraform configurations and provider versions up-to-date to benefit from the latest features and security patches.

Implement alerts

In addition to dashboards, set up alerting to proactively notify your team of any issues across your multicloud environment.

Consider compliance

Ensure that your multicloud monitoring solution meets any compliance requirements specific to your industry or organization.

By leveraging Terraform for deploying a multicloud monitoring solution, you can achieve a more unified view of your infrastructure across different cloud providers, enabling better decision-making and more efficient management of your multicloud environment.

10.10 Automating Disaster Recovery with Terraform and AWS

Problem

Disaster recovery (DR) is a critical aspect of any robust infrastructure strategy. In the event of a disaster or major outage, having a reliable and automated disaster recovery process is essential to minimize downtime and ensure business continuity. However, manually setting up and managing disaster recovery infrastructure can be complex, time-consuming, and prone to errors.

Solution

Terraform provides a way to automate the provisioning and management of disaster recovery infrastructure on AWS. By leveraging Terraform's declarative syntax and AWS services such as Amazon S3, Amazon Elastic Block Store (EBS), and AWS Elastic Disaster Recovery (DRS), you can define and deploy a comprehensive disaster recovery solution.

Here's an example of how to implement an automated disaster recovery solution using Terraform and AWS:

```
provider "aws" {
  region = "us-west-2"  # Primary region
}

provider "aws" {
  alias  = "dr"
  region = "us-east-1"  # DR region
}

# Create S3 bucket for backup storage
resource "aws_s3_bucket" "backup" {
  bucket = "example-dr-backup-bucket"
  acl    = "private"

  versioning {
    enabled = true
  }

  lifecycle_rule {
    enabled = true

    transition {
      days          = 30
      storage_class = "GLACIER"
    }
```

```
    expiration {
      days = 90
    }
  }
}

# Create EC2 instance for the primary site
resource "aws_instance" "primary" {
  ami           = "ami-0c55b159cbfafe1f0"
  instance_type = "t3.micro"

  tags = {
    Name = "primary-instance"
  }
}

# Create EBS volume for data replication
resource "aws_ebs_volume" "primary_data" {
  availability_zone = aws_instance.primary.availability_zone
  size              = 100
  type              = "gp3"

  tags = {
    Name = "primary-data-volume"
  }
}

# Attach EBS volume to the primary instance
resource "aws_volume_attachment" "primary_data_attachment" {
  device_name = "/dev/sdh"
  volume_id   = aws_ebs_volume.primary_data.id
  instance_id = aws_instance.primary.id
}

# Create AWS Elastic Disaster Recovery (DRS) replication configuration
resource "aws_drs_replication_configuration_template" "example" {
  source_server {
    instance_type = "t3.micro"

    tags = {
      Name = "DR-Replica"
    }
  }

  ebs_encryption {
    kms_key_id = aws_kms_key.dr_key.arn
  }
}

# Create KMS key for DR encryption
resource "aws_kms_key" "dr_key" {
  description             = "KMS key for DR encryption"
  deletion_window_in_days = 10
  enable_key_rotation     = true
}

# Create CloudWatch event rule to trigger DR failover
resource "aws_cloudwatch_event_rule" "dr_failover" {
  name        = "dr-failover-trigger"
  description = "Triggers DR failover process"

  event_pattern = jsonencode({
    "source": ["aws.health"],
```

```
    "detail-type": ["AWS Health Event"],
    "detail": {
      "service": ["EC2"],
      "eventTypeCategory": ["issue"],
      "region": ["us-west-2"]
    }
  })
}

# Create Lambda function to handle DR failover
resource "aws_lambda_function" "dr_failover" {
  filename      = "dr_failover_function.zip"
  function_name = "dr-failover-handler"
  role          = aws_iam_role.dr_lambda_role.arn
  handler       = "index.handler"
  runtime       = "nodejs14.x"

  environment {
    variables = {
      DR_CONFIGURATION_ID = aws_drs_replication_configuration_template.example.id
    }
  }
}

# Create IAM role for Lambda function
resource "aws_iam_role" "dr_lambda_role" {
  name = "dr-lambda-role"

  assume_role_policy = jsonencode({
    Version = "2012-10-17"
    Statement = [
      {
        Action = "sts:AssumeRole"
        Effect = "Allow"
        Principal = {
          Service = "lambda.amazonaws.com"
        }
      }
    ]
  })
}

# Attach CloudWatch event to Lambda function
resource "aws_cloudwatch_event_target" "dr_failover" {
  rule      = aws_cloudwatch_event_rule.dr_failover.name
  target_id = "TriggerDRFailover"
  arn       = aws_lambda_function.dr_failover.arn
}
```

Discussion

Automating disaster recovery with Terraform and AWS offers several benefits:

Reproducibility

 The entire DR infrastructure is defined as code, making it easy to re-create or update the setup as needed.

Consistency

 Terraform ensures that the DR environment is consistently provisioned and configured, reducing the risk of human error.

Version control

The DR infrastructure configuration can be version-controlled, providing a history of changes and enabling easy rollbacks if needed.

Automated failover

By using CloudWatch events and Lambda, the failover process can be automated, reducing downtime in case of a disaster.

Cost optimization

With Terraform, you can easily manage the life cycle of DR resources, spinning them up when needed and tearing them down when not in use to optimize costs.

When implementing an automated disaster recovery solution with Terraform, consider the following best practices:

Regular testing

Implement and regularly execute DR drills to ensure that the failover process works as expected.

Data synchronization

Ensure that data is properly replicated between the primary and DR sites. Consider using services like AWS Database Migration Service for database replication.

Network configuration

Properly configure VPCs, subnets, and security groups in both primary and DR regions to ensure seamless failover.

Monitoring and alerting

Implement comprehensive monitoring and alerting to quickly detect issues in both primary and DR environments.

Least privilege

Follow the principle of least privilege when setting up IAM roles and policies for your DR resources.

Documentation

Maintain clear documentation of the DR process, including manual steps if any, to ensure smooth execution during an actual disaster.

Compliance

Ensure that your DR solution meets any compliance requirements specific to your industry or organization.

Cost management

Regularly review and optimize the costs associated with your DR setup, considering services like AWS Savings Plans for long-term cost reduction.

By leveraging Terraform to automate disaster recovery on AWS, you can create a more reliable, repeatable, and efficient DR process, ultimately improving your organization's resilience to potential disasters or major outages.

Index

Symbols

$$\{...\}$ syntax, 61
${...}$ syntax, 61
% (modulo operator), 67

A

abstraction, as benefit of modular configuration, 195
access control
    AWS Secrets Manager, 153, 167
    collaborative workflows, 138
    multienvironment infrastructure, 243
access control, HCP Terraform, 134
Advanced Packaging Tool (APT), 6
alerting
    Auto Scaling group, 246
    compliance violations, 217
    DR infrastructure, 253
alias argument, 99
Amazon CloudWatch, 167, 240
Amazon Managed Grafana, 211-214
Amazon S3, 12
Amazon Virtual Private Cloud (see VPC)
Amazon Web Services (see AWS)
AMI data source, 209
AMP (Amazon Managed Service for Prometheus), 211-214
annotations, adjusting for Kubernetes Deployments, 111-112
Ansible
    configuration management, 175-176
    single-server infrastructure, 3
API Gateway, 237-241
APT (Advanced Packaging Tool), 6

AsciiDoc format, 34
authentication
    for private modules, 81-83
    for providers, 79-81
Auto Scaling group, 244
-auto-approve flag, 136
automated runs, as benefit of HCP Terraform, 138
automation
    Auto Scaling group, 245
    multicloud monitoring, 249
    multienvironment infrastructure, 243
    serverless applications, 239
AWS (Amazon Web Services), 1, 9
    adding and configuring providers, 8
    automating database migrations with RDS, 234-237
    AWS CloudFormation, 3
    disaster recovery automation, 250-254
    EC2 instances
        creating, 83-85
        executing shell scripts on, 174-175
    EKS
        configuring Kubernetes clusters, 104
        deploying Kubernetes clusters, 104
        provisioning scalable clusters, 227-230
    Elastic Load Balancing, 190
    integrating serverless applications with, 240
    Secrets Manager, 152-153
    serverless application deployment on Lambda, 237-241
    Vault, 81
AWS Config, 214-217
aws_db_instance resource, 153

permissions and, 99
idempotency
GitHub repositories, 89
GitHub secrets, 87
migration scripts, 236
implicit dependencies, 188
import block, 183
infrastructure
automating deployment, 2
complex, 2
importing existing, 182-184
limiting potential impact of changes to, 43-45
managing across cloud providers, 2
single server, 3
infrastructure as a service (IaaS), 3
infrastructure as code (see IaC)
input data
error message clarity, 68-70
prefix and suffix removal, 48-49
sanitizing, 47-48
sequential processing, 66-68
validating input strings, 61-63

J

job block, 123
jsondecode function
AWS Secrets Manager, 153
Consul HTTP API, 94
consuming data from HTTP interfaces, 180
jsonencode function, 110

K

k2tf, 109-111
key-values
dynamic configuration with Consul KV, 90-92, 177-178
retrieving from HashiCorp Vault, 153-155
KMS (Key Management Service), 75
Kubernetes, 1
adjusting annotations for Deployments, 111-112
adjusting configuration for Deployments, 112-114
applying NetworkPolicies, 114-117
authorizing Terraform for cluster operations, 105-106
cluster deployment versus configuration, 103-105

converting YAML into HCL, 109-111
Helm
deploying containers with, 117-119
monitoring for Deployments with, 119-122
provisioning scalable clusters using EKS, 227-230
scheduling containers
with HCL, 107-109
with YAML, 106-107
Secrets management
with HashiCorp Vault and Terraform, 157-160
with native functions, 155-157
Pod configuration, 156
kubernetes_deployment resource, 108, 111, 113
kubernetes_manifest resource, 107, 110
kubernetes_network_policy resource, 116
kubernetes_pod resource, 157
kubernetes_secret resource, 157

L

labels, annotations versus, 112
least privilege principle, 83, 217, 240, 253
linting, with GitHub Actions, 76-79
Linux
installing OpenTofu on, 5
installing Terraform on, 4
lists, sorting, 54-55
local Docker images, 101-103
local filesystem interaction, 57-59
local-exec provisioner
simulating postconditions with, 30
lock files, 16
lower() function, 52-54

M

macOS
installing OpenTofu on, 5
installing Terraform on, 4
main.tf file, 84
maintainability
dynamic and flexible configurations, 210
modular configurations, 195
multicloud configurations, 204
Managed Service Identity (MSI), 81
markdown format, terraform-docs command, 34
masked_input local value, 50

About the Authors

Kerim Satirli is a senior developer advocate at HashiCorp, where he coaches operators and developers on sustainable infrastructure and orchestration workflows. Before he joined HashiCorp, Kerim worked on industrial IoT for the Amsterdam airport and helped museums bring more of their collections online. When Kerim isn't working, he's either spending time with his daughter, enjoying aerial photography, or baking a cake.

Taylor Dolezal is the head of ecosystem at the Cloud Native Computing Foundation (CNCF), where he drives innovation and collaboration in the cloud native landscape. Throughout his career, Taylor has been the bridge between complex systems and human understanding, whether through site reliability engineering, developing software solutions, or pairing on innovative technical stacks. When Taylor isn't immersed in the world of cloud native technologies, he's exploring trails around Los Angeles, diving into a good book, and optimizing his pun delivery pipeline for maximum ROI.

Colophon

The animal on the cover of *Terraform Cookbook* is an arctic fox (*Vulpes lagopus*), a small fox common throughout the Arctic tundra of the Northern Hemisphere. The arctic fox is the only land mammal native to Iceland, having walked over the frozen sea to the island at the end of the last ice age.

Well-adapted to cold environments, this fox has thick, warm fur and a large tail. The foxes range in size from 18 to 27 inches long, with a generally round shape to help minimize loss of body heat. They increase their body weight by more than 50% to prepare for winter, when food is scarce. With these adaptations, the foxes don't shiver until the temperature falls to –94 °F.

Arctic foxes live in maze-like dens that generations of foxes use for decades. They mainly prey on lemmings; the fox's reproduction rate is directly related to the lemming population density, which fluctuates every 3–5 years. When food is scarce, the foxes don't reproduce, but when lemmings are abundant, a fox can birth up to 25 pups. The pups emerge from the den by 4 weeks of age and are weaned by 9 weeks.

Although some populations are acutely endangered, the arctic fox's IUCN conservation status is least concern. Many of the animals on O'Reilly covers are endangered; all of them are important to the world.

The cover illustration is by Karen Montgomery, based on an antique line engraving from *Lydekker's Royal Natural History*. The series design is by Edie Freedman, Ellie Volckhausen, and Karen Montgomery. The cover fonts are Gilroy Semibold and Guardian Sans. The text font is Adobe Minion Pro; the heading font is Adobe Myriad Condensed; and the code font is Dalton Maag's Ubuntu Mono.